CAPE PLAYS

LIFE CLASS

DAVID STOREY

# LIFE CLASS

JONATHAN CAPE
THIRTY BEDFORD SQUARE LONDON

FIRST PUBLISHED 1975
© 1975 BY DAVID STOREY

JONATHAN CAPE LTD
30 BEDFORD SQUARE, LONDON WCI

HARDBACK EDITION ISBN 0 224 01083 2
PAPERBACK EDITION ISBN 0 224 01110 3

SET IN 11 PT BEMBO 270 1 PT LEADED

PRINTED IN GREAT BRITAIN
BY EBENEZER BAYLIS AND SON LTD
THE TRINITY PRESS, WORCESTER, AND LONDON

This play was first presented at the Royal Court Theatre, London, on April 9th, 1974, under the direction of Lindsay Anderson. The cast was as follows:

| | |
|---|---|
| Allott | ALAN BATES |
| Warren | STEPHEN BENT |
| Saunders | FRANK GRIMES |
| Stella | ROSEMARY MARTIN |
| Mathews | PAUL KELLY |
| Brenda | SALLY WATTS |
| Carter | DAVID LINCOLN |
| Catherine | GABRIELLE LLOYD |
| Mooney | STEWART RAYNER |
| Gillian | BRENDA CAVENDISH |
| Abercrombie | BOB PECK |
| Foley | BRIAN GLOVER |
| Philips | GERALD JAMES |

# ACT ONE

*A stage.*

*Off-centre, stage right, is a wooden platform, some six to eight feet square, on castors.*

*Beside it are two metal stands, about six feet high, each equipped with two vertical flat-plate heaters. Scattered around the platform are two or three easels and several wooden 'donkeys': low, rectangular stools with an upright T-shaped bar at one end. On one, folded, is a white sheet. There are two brown hessian screens, one upstage centre, the other centre left. Upstage left is a rack with coatpegs.*
ALLOTT *comes in stage left. In his late thirties, medium-build, he wears a duffle-coat, battered trilby hat and gloves. Blows in his hands. Thumps gloves. Shivers. Looks round. Goes over to the wall, switches on the heaters, comes back, takes off gloves, feels plates. Warms one hand, then the other: looks round, puts gloves back on. Steps back. Examines platform, head on one side. Contemplates. Returns to platform: pushes it into new position: contemplates: adjusts it slightly.*

WARREN *comes in: young, well-built: overcoat and scarf. Stays at one side.*

WARREN. Morning, sir.
ALLOTT. Morning, Warren.

(WARREN *watches* ALLOTT *a while adjusting platform.*)
WARREN. ... Nobody else here then, yet, Mr Allott.
ALLOTT (*pays* WARREN *no attention*). Perfectly correct.
WARREN. Er ... cold.
ALLOTT. Very.
WARREN. Get a cup of tea.
ALLOTT. That's right.

WARREN. Well ... See you.

ALLOTT. Hope so.

WARREN. Yeh. (*Last look round: he goes.*)

> (ALLOTT *steps back: contemplates. Goes over to heater: carries it round to the platform's new position.*
>
> SAUNDERS *comes in: thin, anaemic; raincoat, young.*)

SAUNDERS. Morning, sir.

ALLOTT. Saunders.

SAUNDERS. Need any help, sir?

ALLOTT. Let's see. (*Takes off gloves: takes off coat.*) Could hang that up somewhere. (*Then hat.*) And that.

SAUNDERS. Right. (*Takes them.*)

ALLOTT. Er ... Over there, I think ... That's right ... Now, then. Chalk. Pencil. (*Feels in jacket pockets: checks.*) Toilet paper ... Seen Mr Philips, have you?

SAUNDERS. No, sir.

ALLOTT. Had some unfinished business there, I recollect.

SAUNDERS. Anything else, sir?

ALLOTT. No ... Yes. Could chalk the platform. There's a lad. (*Hands him chalk.*)

SAUNDERS. Right.

ALLOTT. Shan't be a sec ... (*Hesitates. Looks round.*) ... Right. (*He goes.*)

> (SAUNDERS *chalks off the corners of the platform on the floor.*
>
> *As he reaches the third corner,* STELLA *comes in: a model, in her twenties: she's muffled up in a heavy coat and cap: carries a shopping-bag as well as a handbag.*)

STELLA. Freezing. (*Shivers: goes directly to the heater.*)

SAUNDERS. Just setting this ...

STELLA. Mr Allott here?

SAUNDERS. He's just gone out ...

STELLA. You wouldn't pop these in the cubicle, would you, love?

SAUNDERS. Yes. (*Takes the bag and handbag.*)

STELLA. Do my shopping on the way up. Get in early ...
Worth all the trouble ... I'll be in the ... Shan't be long.
(*She goes.*)

>    (SAUNDERS *crosses to the upstage screen: takes bags behind.*
>    *Pause.*
>    MATHEWS *comes in: he's followed by* BRENDA.
>    MATHEWS *wears a windcheater. He's smoking.* BRENDA
>    *wears a coat: both are young.*
>    MATHEWS *drops his cigarette, treads it out.*)

MATHEWS. Brenda: have a ride ...

BRENDA. Not likely ... Been on there before.

>    (MATHEWS *pushes the platform like a trolley: jumps on for*
>    *a ride: screams out.*)

MATHEWS. Smashing ...

SAUNDERS (*coming back*). Here ... I'm just marking that.
(*He takes the platform from* MATHEWS *and pushes it*
*back.*)

BRENDA (*to* SAUNDERS). Allott here, then, is he?

SAUNDERS. Yeh.

MATHEWS. Gone down to the bog. I bet he has ... Spends
bloody hours in there, he does.

BRENDA. Not the only one, I think.

MATHEWS. Writes bloody poetry ... Ask Warren ...
Saunders: isn't that right?

SAUNDERS. You've made a mess of this ... I can't find the
other mark.

MATHEWS. Come on. Come on. Over here ... that's right.
(*Helps him.*)

BRENDA. So cold ... (*Shivers, standing by the heater.*) Shan't
do anything today ... Just look ... Can hardly hold a
pencil. Dropping off. (*Holds up her hands.*)

MATHEWS. Ought to walk here.

BRENDA. Walk here?

A* 9

MATHEWS. Do you good ... I walk every morning, as a matter of fact.

BRENDA. I've seen you.

MATHEWS. Eyes'll drop out one day.

BRENDA. Tell her you're an artist, do you?

MATHEWS. Don't need to tell her ... Can tell it at a glance.

BRENDA. Here. Saunders. Should have seen him. Mathews — walking: hand in hand.

MATHEWS. What's matter with hand in hand?

BRENDA. Your grubby hands ... You want to wash them.

MATHEWS. A damn sight cleaner, love, than yours. (*Grapples with her: takes her.*)

BRENDA. Get off! ... Go on! ... *Get off!*

CARTER (*entering*). Here. Here. Here. What's going on in here?

> (CARTER *is small, stocky, genial: dressed in jeans and a zip-jacket, young.*)

MATHEWS. She's molesting me, Kenneth ... Ever since I came in ... Follows me around. Just look.

> (*Having been released by* MATHEWS *at* CARTER'*s entrance,* BRENDA *has followed him around to hit him back: now, however, she moves off.*)

CARTER. Allott here, then, is he?

MATHEWS. In the bog.

CARTER. Ay ... is it true, then? Sits in there ... who told me?

MATHEWS. Warren ...

CARTER. Writing verses in a book.

> (MATHEWS *laughs.*)

BRENDA. What's the matter with writing that?

MATHEWS. Shan't say a word ... (*Moves off. Then:*) Should read some of it, my love.

BRENDA. Better than the stuff you write ... Did you hear that Foley caught him writing on the stairs?

CARTER. Here ...

BRENDA. On the wall.

SAUNDERS. What was that, then, Mathews?

CARTER. Go on, then. What did he say?

MATHEWS. Nothing ...

CARTER. Come on. Come on, then. (*To* BRENDA) What did he write?

BRENDA. Dunno ... Had to wash it off.

MATHEWS. Bloody obsessionalist, that man ... Should see a doctor.

CARTER. Come on ... Come on ... When was it?

BRENDA. Aren't you going to tell us, Bryan?

MATHEWS. Tell you bloody nothing ... Mouth like a gramophone. Yak, yak, yak ...

BRENDA. 'Mr Foley is feeling poorly': that's the sort of stuff he used to write.

CARTER. Brenda: how about it, love? (*Embraces her: sway together.*)

SAUNDERS. I've marked that platform: nobody move it.

CARTER. Shan't touch it. No. We shan't. We shan't. (*Hums to himself: sways with* BRENDA.)

(MATHEWS *picks spots on his face, standing resentfully to one side.*)

BRENDA (*sings*). Have you ever ...
Asked me whether ...

CARTER (*sings*). No, I've never ...
Asked you whether.

BRENDA (*sings*). I would ever ...

CARTER (*sings*). You would ever ...

BRENDA (*sings*). Dance the whole night long with you!

(*They laugh, embracing.*
CATHERINE *comes in: late teens: dressed in a long coat and cap; carries a large straw bag. Panting, sets down her bag by a donkey: takes off cap.*)

CATHERINE. Run up all those stairs ... Do it every morning. Exercise, you know.

MATHEWS. Could run up somewhere else with me, love. (*Guffaws.*)

> (CATHERINE *glances over: otherwise disregarding: takes off gloves.*
>
> BRENDA *has disengaged herself from* CARTER: *she crosses over to* CATHERINE.)

BRENDA. Did you bring it with you?

CATHERINE. Here, then: have a look.

> (*She gets a hat from the straw bag: tries it on for* BRENDA'S *approval.*
>
> MATHEWS *crosses over to* CARTER.)

CARTER. Got a fag?

MATHEWS. Last one.

CARTER. Sammy?

SAUNDERS. Got a pipe.

MATHEWS. Joking.

SAUNDERS. No, then ... (*Gets one out: puts it in his mouth.*)

MATHEWS. Here ... (*Takes it: tries it in his own mouth.*) How d'I look?

CARTER (*ignoring* MATHEWS). How long have you had a pipe, then, Sammy?

SAUNDERS. A week or two ... Smoke it in the evenings.

CARTER. Evenings.

SAUNDERS. Just before I go to bed.

MATHEWS. Do summat else, personally, just afore I go to bed. (*Laughs, pipe between his teeth.*)

> (CARTER *takes the pipe from him and gives it back to* SAUNDERS.
>
> WARREN *comes in, dressed as before.*)

WARREN. Somebody's got here, then, have they? Be half of 'em away today.

CARTER. Seen Allott, have you?

WARREN. Yeh. Came in before ... Morning, Brenda ... Morning, Catherine.

BRENDA *and* CATHERINE (*together*). Morning, Warren.

WARREN. Nice day for it. What d'you think?

BRENDA. Lovely.

WARREN. That your hat, then?

(BRENDA *has now tried it.*)

BRENDA. Catherine's.

CATHERINE. Do you like it?

WARREN. Dunno ... (CATHERINE *tries it.*) Suits her. (*Indicating* CATHERINE.)

BRENDA. Thank you. Just what I was hoping.

MATHEWS. Here ... give us a try, then, love. (*Snatches it from her head.*)

CATHERINE. Come here ... Give it back ... It cost a lot of money did that hat ... (*Walks after him as* MATHEWS *dances away, the hat on his head.*)

MATHEWS. Here ... here ... How d'I look?

BRENDA. Give it back ...

MATHEWS. Come and get it ... Sammy: how d'I look? (*Dances on to the platform.*)

ALLOTT (*entering*). You the new model, are you, Mathews ... ? bit over to the right. Lovely ... Lower your trousers and I think we'll be all right.

(*They all laugh:* MATHEWS *gets down moodily from the platform.*

CATHERINE *takes her hat.*)

Spend more time getting ready for what you have to do ... turning your thoughts to higher things ... time and space ... the eternal verities ... wouldn't do you any harm. Your hat, is it, Catherine?

CATHERINE. Yes, sir.

ALLOTT. Very nice ... (*To* SAUNDERS) Stella arrived, then, has she?

SAUNDERS. Yes, sir ... Said she wouldn't be long.

CARTER. Composed any poems this morning, sir?

ALLOTT. What?

MATHEWS. Poems, sir.

> (*The girls giggle.*
> ALLOTT *pauses. Then:*)

ALLOTT. If we could have a little application ... tools of the trade ... Catherine: I should put away your hat.

> (DEREK MOONEY *and* GILLIAN STAFFORD *come in.*
> MOONEY *has long hair.* GILLIAN *is slender.*)

MOONEY. Are we late, sir?

ALLOTT. No, no, Mooney. Just in time ... Gillian.

GILLIAN. Morning, sir.

ALLOTT. Looks to me as if half our members are going to be away today ... Colds. 'Flu ... Distemper ... Myxomatosis ... What do you think, Carter?

CARTER. Yes, sir. Weather like this.

ALLOTT. Seen anyone on your travels, Mooney?

MOONEY. No, sir.

ALLOTT. Except Gillian, of course.

MOONEY. Yes, sir.

ALLOTT. One day I'll find one of you two alone.

WARREN. What will you do then, sir?

ALLOTT. I shall tell—the him or her as the case may be—certain relevant facts, Warren.

WARREN. What about, sir?

ALLOTT. Facts which may well lead—the him or her as the case may be—to revise their opinion about the other ... him or her, as the case may be.

CARTER. Tell us now, sir.

BRENDA. What secrets have you got, sir?

ALLOTT. Sammy: everything in order, is it?

SAUNDERS. Yes, sir.

MOONEY. What facts are they, sir?

CATHERINE. Gillian's dying to know, sir!

ALLOTT. It's you, Mooney, I'm worried about ... Has it ever struck you, for instance, that you've another fifty or sixty years to live?

MOONEY. Yes, sir.

ALLOTT. How about you, Gillian?

GILLIAN. Yes, sir.

ALLOTT. Doesn't that come as a terrible shock?

GILLIAN. No, sir.

ALLOTT. You'll be tired of this long-haired ninny by the time short hair comes in again.

MOONEY. I'll get it cut.

ALLOTT. She won't love you with it cut. Will you, Gilly?

GILLIAN. I don't know ... I like it long.

MOONEY. Here, sir ... !

ALLOTT. Sammy: how about these stools?

SAUNDERS. Yes, sir.

ALLOTT. Paper: pencils: ink ... (*Sees* MOONEY *still waiting.*) Ipso facto, Mooney.

MOONEY. Yes, sir. (*Apprehensive: after exchanging looks with* GILLIAN, *slowly goes.*)

(*The others wander off, except* CATHERINE, *who gets a large drawing-block from her straw bag, and* GILLIAN, *who has brought her board with her.*

STELLA *comes on in a dressing-gown.*)

STELLA. Thought I'd change in the loo today. Warmer ... (*Shivers: goes to the platform: feels the heater: warms her hands.*) Gillian ... How's Derek?

GILLIAN. All right, Stella.

STELLA. Wish I was young again.

ALLOTT. You are young.

STELLA. Really, *youthful* young.

ALLOTT. You are *youthful* young ... as young as anybody ought to be round here ... All these *aficionados*—myopic ...

disingenuous ... uninspired—are images of youth no longer: pubescent excrescences on the cheeks of time.

GILLIAN. Oh, sir!

(ALLOTT *has taken the white cloth from the donkey and crosses to the throne.*)

CATHERINE. In any case, study of natural objects isn't very popular today, sir.

ALLOTT. What?

CATHERINE. The study of natural objects.

ALLOTT. Are you a natural object, Stella?

STELLA. Don't feel like one ... Least, not natural.

CATHERINE. I mean, anything that's real.

ALLOTT. Stella's real ... Then again, in another sense, you could say she's quite unearthly.

(ALLOTT *arranges the white cloth on the throne.*)

CATHERINE. It's more, nowadays, doing what you feel.

ALLOTT. What do you feel, Catherine?

CATHERINE. More expressing ... sort of ... whatever it is.

(ALLOTT *waits.*)

Well ... sort of ...

(*Waits.*)

I'm speaking, sort of ... about it all in general.

ALLOTT. I see.

(BRENDA *comes back in with drawing-board, etc.*)

I can't ask Gillian, of course ... Never known anyone feel so much with so little to show for it—except that unearthly bloody freak.

(MOONEY *is returning with board and paper.*)

CATHERINE. Sir!

BRENDA. She's sensitive, she is ... aren't you, love?

GILLIAN. Yeh.

BRENDA. She feels it all the time.

GILLIAN. That's right.

16

MATHEWS (*re-entering*). Here. Anybody seen my pencil?
    (*The girls laugh.*)
  Had it in me locker. Pack o' thieves round here ... Can't
  put anything down.

BRENDA. No need to look in this direction.

CATHERINE. Accuse anybody, he would.

GILLIAN. Have you looked inside your pockets?

MATHEWS. Want to look in there, then, for me?

GILLIAN. Wouldn't look in there, not if they paid me.

MATHEWS. Not like some of the birds I know.

STELLA. Here, then ... How do you want me? Standing up
  today, or sitting down?

ALLOTT. Standing up, I think, to start ... Recumbent
  yesterday, I recollect ... Had the second years in. My God
  ... Licentious. To a man.
    (MATHEWS *guffaws hugely.*
    ALLOTT *circles the platform, chin in hand, contemplating
    the empty space.*
    STELLA *waits.*
    CARTER *and* WARREN *have come back in.*)

WARREN. Saw Abercrombie on the stairs ... come in a
  bowler hat, he has.

ALLOTT. What's that? (*Studies throne.*)

WARREN. Come in a bowler hat, sir.
    (*The girls laugh.*)

ALLOTT. I could do with a bowler hat ... Gave hints at
  birthday time ... what do I get? A box of pencils.

CATHERINE. Artist, sir.

ALLOTT. I have other interests, you know, as well.

MATHEWS. What're they, then, sir? (*He laughs, looking at the
  others.*)

CARTER. Young ladies.

BRENDA *and* CATHERINE (*together*). Sir!

ALLOTT. Oh, I keep my eye open, Catherine ... not very much here escapes my notice.

GILLIAN. I thought you were married, sir.

ALLOTT. I am married ... I've been married in fact for a very considerable time ... In fact, the longer I stay married the more appreciative I become ...

> Oh, he loved form,
> And he loved beauty—
> But above all else
> He knew his duty.

CATHERINE. Oh, sir!

ALLOTT.
> He called for fruit,
> He called for wine:
> He called for love—
> But that took time.

BRENDA. Go on, sir. That's super.

ALLOTT.
> 'I'll dream of you,' she said:
> '*All life is a fantasy:*
> We create illusions, call them love:'
> Pray sing to me, my dove.

CARTER. Anything else, sir?

ALLOTT. No, no. That's sufficient, I think, to be going on with.

MATHEWS. What other interests have you got, sir?

ALLOTT. Fishing.

MATHEWS. Fishing! (*Laughs.*)

ALLOTT. You interested in fishing, Mathews?

MATHEWS. Not half, sir! (*Laughs.*) Things I go fishing for you don't catch in ponds. (*Laughs.*)

ALLOTT. Where do you catch them, Mathews, if it's not too much to ask?

WARREN. In his bleeding pockets.

CARTER. *Dirty bugger.*

MOONEY. *Dirty sod.*

MATHEWS. Piss off!
>    (*The others laugh.*)
ALLOTT. Now, now ... Stella here's quite shocked ... Never
>    knew they spoke like that, did you, Stell?
STELLA. Hear some things here I'd never hear anywhere
>    else.
MATHEWS. Ears like that I'm not surprised.
ALLOTT. Here ... Here. Now apologize for that. (*Waits.*)
>    (*Pause:* MATHEWS *struggles with himself.*)
MATHEWS. I apologize, Stella. Very much.
STELLA. That's all right.
MATHEWS. Give you a kiss, then? Make up.
STELLA. No need to go as far as that, I'm sure.
CARTER. Go a damn sight farther, if he had a chance.
ALLOTT. To your stools, men.
>    (*Guffaw from* MATHEWS, CARTER, WARREN.)
>  Cathy: close the door. Saunders: let's have the screen
>  to stop the draught.
>    (*They move to the stools and easels,* CATHERINE *to the
>    entrance, stage left,* SAUNDERS *to the screen, centre left:
>    arranges it.* STELLA *climbs on to the throne: disrobes.*
>    CARTER *whistles.*)
STELLA (*smiles, waiting to be posed*). Enough. Enough.
WARREN. Why don't you take it off more slowly?
STELLA. Not for you ... I only do that, you know, for friends.
>    (*Whistles, catcalls:* ALLOTT *sets the pose: standing.*)
ALLOTT. Left ... Arm ... More sort of ... Right one ...
>    (STELLA *follows his instructions.*)
>  That's it ... Comfortable?
STELLA. Yeh.
>    (ALLOTT *chalks her feet: blue chalk which he takes from
>    his pocket, marking the white sheet.*)
MATHEWS. Watch your toes, there, darling.
STELLA. Watch your something else, my love.

MATHEWS. Oh. Oh. Hear that ... Everything's under control. (*Examines his flies.*) Yes ... yes. Look. Quite nice. Quite lovely.

CARTER. Dirty bugger.

MOONEY. Dirty sod.

ALLOTT. Right, then, Leonardos ... On your marks, get set ...

    (MATHEWS *blows raspberry.*)

ALLOTT. Go.

    (*Laughter: fades slowly:*

    *they start drawing.* SAUNDERS *comes back from setting the screen.* CATHERINE *is already back.*

    *Each has different mannerisms:*

    WARREN *stands, straight back, sturdy, draws with charcoal: thick, simple lines: few, much pondered.*

    SAUNDERS *uses various aids: hangs plumb-line from strut of stool to squint past: ruler to hold up at arm's length, one eye closed, to gaze at the proportions of Stella: rubber, set-square, penknife: makes numerous dots and marks, as if about to plot a map.*

    MATHEWS *draws scruffily, ostentatiously, careless, with numerous scratching movements, scarcely looking at the model, occasionally gasping at errors, or his own performance.*

    BRENDA *draws in a similar fashion, but less ostentatiously. Much head-waving from side to side, with odd glances at the model, more to see if she's there, it seems, rather than by way of examination.*

    CARTER *stands straight-backed, like Warren, but draws a neat, well-observed, meticulous figure, unimaginative, pain-staking, unengaged.*

    CATHERINE *draws in ink: a somewhat dotted figure, like plotting out a graph: much head-waving too, with frequent — if brief — glances at Stella: the marks she makes are scarcely visible.*

MOONEY *draws an idealized figure: rather like a large banana, smooth, formless, simplified almost to abstraction: studies the model conscientiously.*

GILLIAN *is expressionistic: enjoys drawing: puts a great deal of feeling into it, apparently; yet the result is light, sketchy, almost inconsequential.*

ALLOTT, *after marking off the corners of the cloth on the platform with his blue chalk, walks round a moment, studying the model himself, casually, disinterested.*)

MATHEWS. Here. Go on. Lend us it.

SAUNDERS. Use your own.

MATHEWS. I haven't got one.

ALLOTT. What is it, Marvel?

MATHEWS. Rubber, sir. Saunders. Won't let me have it.

ALLOTT (*looks*). There's nothing there.

MATHEWS. Is, sir. There, sir.

(ALLOTT *stoops down to* MATHEWS' *drawing from behind* MATHEWS' *back.*)

There.

ALLOTT. Soot.

MATHEWS. No, sir! Made a mistake, sir.

ALLOTT. Lend him it, Saunders. Last time ... Don't want to see any rubbers after this.

ALL. Oh, sir!

ALLOTT. Draw. Draw. That's all you're here to do.

CARTER. What if we make a mistake, sir?

ALLOTT. Draw round it, underneath it. Makes no difference in the end ... *What is true will last* ... What is real — Gillian and Mooney — is eternal.

GILLIAN. Oh, sir.

MATHEWS. Been busy already, hasn't he, Sammy?

(ALLOTT *looks across.*)

Poetical composition, sir.

(WARREN, CARTER, BRENDA *laugh.*)

ALLOTT.                  Oh time is space
                                    And space is distance,
                                    Distance time
                                    And time consuming ...

BRENDA. Sir!

ALLOTT. Don't want to see how much, Mathews, just—how well.

MATHEWS. Sir.

ALLOTT. Very nice, Catherine.

CATHERINE. Thank you, sir.

ALLOTT. Fewer calculations, more intuition, Sammy: not a mathematical problem.

SAUNDERS. Yes, sir.

MATHEWS. Mathematical problem to Sammy. Isn't that right?

ALLOTT. Can't draw and talk ... Can't demonstrate, imbibe, celebrate, Stella's peculiar beauty if you're yakketing all the time.

> (ABERCROMBIE *comes in with an electric kettle. Same age as* ALLOTT: *tall, wears a polo-neck sweater, scarf with tassels, gloves, and a bowler hat.*)

ABERCROMBIE. Anybody in?

ALLOTT. Sure.

ABERCROMBIE. Stella.

STELLA. Morning, Mr Abercrombie.

MATHEWS. Morning, Mr Abercrombie.

ABERCROMBIE. Clip your ear, Warren.

MATHEWS. *Mathews*, sir!

ABERCROMBIE. Clip both your ears, Mathews.

MATHEWS. *Sir!*

ABERCROMBIE. Mind if I plug in, old sport?

> (ALLOTT *gestures to him to go ahead.*
> ABERCROMBIE *glances at the drawings, then at* STELLA, *as he passes: goes to the wall: plugs in kettle.*)

ABERCROMBIE. Damn cold.

ALLOTT. Very.

ABERCROMBIE. Pimples. (*Indicates* STELLA. *To* STELLA)
Goose-pimples.

STELLA. All over.

ABERCROMBIE (*to room*). Don't miss any out.

ALL. Oh, sir.

ABERCROMBIE. How's bis?

ALLOTT. All right.

ABERCROMBIE. Half mine away ... God. (*Sneezes hugely:
produces handkerchief: blows.*)

CATHERINE. Like your hat, sir.

ABERCROMBIE. Thank you, Catherine ... Lends an air of
distinction. (*To* ALLOTT) What d'you think?

ALLOTT. Not seen Philips, have you?

ABERCROMBIE. No ... (*To* STELLA) Looking your splendid
self, my dear.

STELLA. Thank you.

ABERCROMBIE. By God: ten years younger ... be doing a
drawing there meself.

STELLA. Wonder what I'm missing.

ABERCROMBIE. My young days, young lady, wouldn't have
to wonder.

STELLA. Ooooh!

ABERCROMBIE. By God. What? ... Might come in and do an
etching ... Not seen Foley round about?

(ALLOTT *shakes his head.*)

Smell his bloody pipe, but canna see the man. (*Shivers.
Slaps his hands together.*) Come cycling in the other
morning ... found Foley parking his car by the rear
entrance to the furnace room. Says: 'This area is reserved
for artisans, Mr Abercrombie, not for members of the
teaching staff.' 'I was parking my bike here, Mr Foley,
sir,' I said. 'Bike or no bike, this is for coke, not for

members of the staff ... ' gesticulating then to his own automated load of refuse and adding, 'If I leave that on the street I get a parking ticket, so the Principal's car's excluded. All transport apart from that has to find its own parking area. I'd be much obliged.'

ALLOTT. You wheeled it out.

ABERCROMBIE. I rode it into college—left it by his door ... Never said a word ... made my point. Subsequently hid it discreetly by the furnace ... where I was this morning when a roar—not unlike a thousand kettles dropped at random by some insidiously careless hand—assailed my ears ... bob down ... raise my head ... cautiously ... find, though the symphony's subsided, the elements as it were are still around ... Foley ... pink-cheeked, perspiring—*the boot of his car wide open*—stooping to the coke and—not lifting in huge handfuls—but *individual pieces* ... after which he wipes his hand, lowers the boot, looks round, walks briskly—very much as if he's accomplished a feat of unparalleled dexterity and daring—up the steps to the college entrance.

ALLOTT. What's he want the coke for?

ABERCROMBIE. Fire.

ALLOTT. In his car?

ABERCROMBIE. At home.

ALLOTT. He'll not get much fire with that.

ABERCROMBIE. Suppose he picks up pieces every day ... after a week ... a month ... a year ... the mind boggles, Allott. He may even, in his leisure hours, run a domestic fuel business ... his house surrounded by veritable mountains of first-grade coke ...

(MATHEWS *has had his hand up for several seconds.*)

MATHEWS. Sir? ...

(ALLOTT *looks up.*)

Can I be excused, sir?

ALLOTT. What for?

MATHEWS (*after some hesitation, and looking round at the others*). I want to go, sir.

ALLOTT. Where?

MATHEWS. To the bog, sir.

ALLOTT. What do you want to do there?

(*Snort from* WARREN.)

MATHEWS. Sir! I've had some medicine, sir.

ALLOTT. What medicine?

MATHEWS (*hesitates. Then:*) To make me go, sir.

ALLOTT. Go ...? You haven't even come.

(*Laughter.*)

MATHEWS. I'll have to go, sir. I've brought a note from my mother.

CARTER. He hasn't got a mother, sir.

MATHEWS. I've got a father.

BRENDA. Different one each day.

MATHEWS. I'll have to go, sir!

MOONEY. Dirty bugger.

WARREN. Dirty sod.

MATHEWS. Sir!

ALLOTT. Two minutes.

MATHEWS. Sir!

ALLOTT. Two minutes.

MATHEWS. *Sir!*

ALLOTT. You can do all you've got to do inside two minutes.

MATHEWS. Sir ...

(MOONEY *calls to him behind his hand as he passes him to the door.*)

*Piss off!* (*Goes.*)

(*The room subsides: the students return to work.*)

STELLA. There's a draught somewhere.

WARREN. That's Mathews. (*Raspberry.*)

(*Laughter.*)

25

ALLOTT. There's no window open, Stella ... And the door is firmly closed. (*Glances behind screen.*) It is.

STELLA. I can still feel it.

WARREN. What's it feel like, Lovely?

STELLA. Nothing you might mind.

ALLOTT. Where do you feel it, Stella ...?

STELLA. Sort of ... down my side.

ALLOTT. Which side?

STELLA. ... My left side, really.

CARTER. That's not a draught ... That's Sammy. (*Indicates* SAUNDERS: *fixed, scrupulous examination of* STELLA.)
(*Laughter.*)

ALLOTT. All right, I'll shift it.
(*Goes to one of the two vertical heaters: moves it slightly, adjusting its position.*)

CATHERINE. Oh, sir!

BRENDA. Oh, *sir*!

CATHERINE. I've drawn it, sir!

BRENDA. *I*'ve drawn it, sir.

ALLOTT. Draw it again.

CATHERINE. I've drawn it *there*, sir!

ALLOTT. Draw it here, then ... How do you think Degas drew his horses ... drew his *ballet-dancers*, Catherine?

CATHERINE. Who, sir?

ALLOTT. Degas.

GILLIAN. Was he a Negro, sir?

ALLOTT. No, he wasn't a Negro.

WARREN. Perhaps he took photographs, sir.

ALLOTT. The moving of an electric heater isn't going to jeopardize your drawing unduly ... (*Looks.*) There's nothing there ...

CATHERINE. There is, sir!

ALLOTT. Shift it.

CATHERINE. Sir: there'll be three of them.

ALLOTT. Better than two ... (*To* ABERCROMBIE) Most revolutions are the result of quite arbitrary decisions taken, invariably, by people not in the least involved.

WARREN. I wouldn't mind taking one or two snapshots ... Certain aspects of Stella are very photogenic.

STELLA. Thank you.

ALLOTT (*to* WARREN). Put away your dirty looks: get on with your dirty drawing.

MOONEY. Got cramp, sir.

ALLOTT. Where?

MOONEY. Finger, sir.

ALLOTT. Massage it.

RRENDA. Ooooh, sir!

CATHERINE. You are awful.

ALLOTT. Get on with it ... ! Drive an angel to distraction ... Draw, for God's sake, draw!

(*They draw.*)

Your kettle finished?

ABERCROMBIE. Boiled and re-boiled, old boy.

ALLOTT. Saunders, haven't you sharpened that pencil enough by now?

(SAUNDERS *goes on sharpening his pencil: he's been sharpening since* CARTER's *reference to him.*)

BRENDA. He's crying, sir.

SAUNDERS. I'm not.

CATHERINE. He was, sir ...

BRENDA. It's what Ken said about him, sir ...

(GILLIAN *has got up and gone to console* SAUNDERS, *arm round his shoulder.*)

GILLIAN. Oh, you're all right, aren't you, Sammy?

ALLOTT. And what was Carter saying about him?

CATHERINE. About Stella feeling the draught, sir.

ALLOTT. For God's sake, leave him alone, girl ... Saunders, put your penknife away and draw.

GILLIAN. I was only consoling him, sir.

ALLOTT. You can console him after hours.

BRENDA. *Sir!*

ALLOTT. It's not a clinic, you know. It's not a haven of rest … It's where the embryonic artist may experience — perhaps for the very first time in his life, Brenda — the faint flutterings of his restless spirit.

CATHERINE. Oh, sir!

ALLOTT. Get on with it, for Christ's sake.

(GILLIAN *goes back reluctantly to her place.*)

When you've finished picking your nose, Carter, you can go with Mr Abercrombie and ask him for a cup of coffee. I'm parched.

CARTER. Yes, sir.

(*Gets up promptly: waits.*)

ABERCROMBIE. Right … (*Hesitates.*) Yes. Well, after all. That's what I came for … Kenneth, is it?

CARTER. Yes, sir.

ABERCROMBIE. Right. We'll make Mr Allott's coffee right away … Two sugars …

ALLOTT. One.

ABERCROMBIE. White …

ALLOTT. Black.

ABERCROMBIE (*to* CARTER). Black. One sugar. (*Goes.*)

(CARTER *follows.*

*Pause. Silence.*

MOONEY *whistles a tune contentedly to himself: low, light.*

ALLOTT, *after calming, has begun to wander slowly round the back of the stools, glancing at the drawings.*

*Apart from the whistling, the room is silent. Then:*)

ALLOTT. Musician.

(*Pause.*)

MOONEY. What?

ALLOTT. Tune.

MOONEY. Oh.

ALLOTT. Preferably silent. (*Indicates the room.*) More creative.

MOONEY. Oh. (*Goes on with his drawing.*)

(ALLOTT *gazes at* MOONEY'S *drawing. Then:*)

ALLOTT. Draw that with your eyes shut?

MOONEY. What ...

ALLOTT. Idealized.

MOONEY. What ...?

ALLOTT. Stella's breasts ...

ALL. *Ooooh!*

ALLOTT. ... are not like water melons hanging from a tree.

CATHERINE. Sir!

ALLOTT. They're global masses, but not conceived, as it were, Mooney, on a global scale.

MOONEY. Oh.

ALLOTT. A weight-lifter might find those thighs something of an encumbrance, Mooney ... It's not a beauty contest, Mooney.

CATHERINE (*having come over to examine the drawing*). Oooh, sir ... Honestly!

ALLOTT. Get back to your seat, young woman.

CATHERINE (*returning*). You ought to see what he's drawn, Jilly.

BRENDA. Better not.

WARREN. Cop a handful of them each evening.

GILLIAN. Shut your mouth.

WARREN. Tits the size of Windsor Castle. (*Standing, peering over.*) Cor blimey ... get the Eiffel Tower between two o' them.

MOONEY. Piss off.

BRENDA (*to* WARREN). Upset him.

MOONEY. Piss off you as well.

ALLOTT. It's just a question ... (*Waits: they quieten, return to drawing.*) It's merely a question, Mooney, of seeing each detail in relation to all the rest ... When you examine the breasts you've to bear in mind, also, the shape and volume of the head, of the chest structure beneath it, of the abdomen in general ... the proportion—the width as well as the height—of the legs: the whole contained, as it were ... (*Looks up: snigger from* WARREN. *Silence. Return to drawing.*) ... within a single image. Unless you are constantly relating the specific to the whole, Mooney ... (WARREN *sniggers*.) ... a work of art can never exist ... It's not merely a conscious effort (*Gazing at the others.*); it is, if one is an artist and not merely a technician—someone disguised, that is, as an artist, going through all the motions and creating all the effects—an instinctive process ... the gift, as it were, of song ... For, after all, a bird sings in its tree (WARREN *and* BRENDA *snigger.*) but doesn't contemplate its song ... similarly the artist sings *his* song, but doesn't contemplate its beauty, doesn't analyse, doesn't lay it out in all its separate parts ... that is the task of the critic, the mechanic ... even of the poseur, the man masquerading as the artist ... the *manufacturer* of events who, in his twentieth-century romantic role, sees art as something accessible to all and therefore the prerogative not of the artist—but of anybody who cares to pick up a brush, a bag of cement, an acetylene welder ... anyone, in fact, who can persuade other people that what he is doing is creative ... That, after all, is the lesson we must learn, Mooney ... That's the lesson we've been convened, as it were, to celebrate ... that we are life's musicians ... its singers, and that what we sing is wholly without meaning ... it exists, merely, because it is ... The one significant distinction between the artist and the scientist, indeed, between him and all his fellow men ... What the artist does is purposeless. That's its dignity ... its beauty.

CATHERINE. I've run out of ink.

ALLOTT. Well, use pencil.

CATHERINE. I've got some in my locker.

ALLOTT. Well, go and get it then.

CATHERINE. Oh, thank you, sir. (*Goes quickly.*)

WARREN. She's gone for a fag: that's what she's gone for.

ALLOTT. Smoking in the studios, Warren, isn't allowed.

WARREN. She'll smoke it in the bog.

GILLIAN. Mr Foley inspects the ladies lavatories regularly: she'll not smoke anything there.

WARREN. *Dirty bugger.*

MOONEY. *Dirty sod.*

ALLOTT. Commemoration of the human spirit and human hygiene often go hand in hand, Mooney.

MOONEY. It wasn't me, sir. It was him.

ALLOTT. Human hygiene and commemoration of the human spirit often go hand in hand, Warren.

WARREN. Yes, sir.

ALLOTT. Did you get that, Warren?

WARREN. Yes, sir.

ALLOTT. I'd hate you to overlook it.

WARREN. Yes, sir.

ALLOTT (*to* GILLIAN).

>               Oh, love will run its course,
>               Come finally to rest,
>               And panting, reined in,
>               Stand waiting for its test.

GILLIAN. Super, sir!

ALLOTT. Thank you, Gillian.

CATHERINE (*returning, breathless*). Got it, sir. (*Begins drawing immediately.*)

ALLOTT (*to* WARREN). Ink is what she wanted: ink is what she got.

WARREN. Yes, sir.

ALLOTT. A man's faith, Warren, is seldom easily come by.

WARREN. No, sir.

ALLOTT. The greatest harm one human being can do to another is to seek to disillusion him ... some people take longer, for instance, to fill their pens than others.

WARREN. Yes, sir.

ALLOTT. And some, of course, never need to fill their pens at all.

WARREN. No, sir.

(MOONEY *and* BRENDA *snigger.*)

ALLOTT. Is that a mystery figure, Brenda? ... Have we—at the end of the day—to decide what it is, where it came from, and who its antecedents are?

BRENDA. No, sir.

ALLOTT. Unformed. Wouldn't you say that's a reasonable assessment, Brenda?

BRENDA. No, sir.

ALLOTT. What Mooney's has got a superabundance of, yours has got none at all.

CATHERINE. It's different for a girl, sir.

ALLOTT. How do you mean?

CATHERINE. Well, sir ...

BRENDA. Drawing breasts, sir.

GILLIAN. Yeh.

CATHERINE. It's different for a girl.

BRENDA. If we'd got a feller to draw it'd be different, sir.

CATHERINE. We could get going with a feller, sir.

WARREN. Hang one on him three feet long.

MOONEY. *Dirty bugger.*

WARREN. *Dirty sod.*

ALLOTT. Warren—*if* you're doing anything at all, that is—it's of far greater interest to me than any of these diverting comments you feel constrained to make from time to time. (*Waits.*) Get on with it.

32

WARREN. It's sexual discrimination, sir.

ALLOTT. There's no sexual discrimination here ... Art is above sex ... and it's above politics, too. That's to say, it absorbs sex, and it absorbs politics.

BRENDA. Why're we always drawing women, then?

ALLOTT. You're not always drawing women.

GILLIAN. We are in here.

CATHERINE. That's sexual discrimination. That's what I mean.

ALLOTT. We had a man once. I remember distinctly.

WARREN. Gave 'em all a shock, sir ... Shoulda seen it. Almost to his knee-caps, sir.

GILLIAN. S'only nature.

CATHERINE. Yeh. It's only nature.

BRENDA. That's what I mean ... Just once.

ALLOTT. We're not here to seek sexual stimulation, Catherine. We're here to peruse a beautiful and seemingly mysterious object, and to set it down—curiously—as objectively as we can.

BRENDA. It's alus a woman, sir.

SAUNDERS. Women have always been the subject of the very greatest art.

   (*Pause: they look at* SAUNDERS.)

Because all the greatest artists, you see, have always been men.

GILLIAN. We know why, don't we, Sammy?

ALLOTT. I don't know why. Have you some information on the subject you've been keeping back from us, Jilly?

GILLIAN. They like contemplating their human slaves.

WARREN. What slaves?

SAUNDERS. Who's a slave?

GILLIAN. Us. We're slaves.

MOONEY. Who keeps you in slavery?

GILLIAN. You do.

MOONEY. Me?

CATHERINE. *Men.*

WARREN. Bollocks.

GILLIAN. That's a man's answer to everything ... *Bollocks.*

MOONEY. I don't like women swearing ... I've told you that before.

GILLIAN. Piss off!

BRENDA. Ooooh, Jilly!

WARREN. They're a pain in the arse, sir. They are, honestly.

SAUNDERS. If women wanted to be artists they've more time than anybody else.

BRENDA. Rubbish ...

CATHERINE. Bollocks!

(*The girls laugh.*)

WARREN. Cor blimey ... sat on their backsides all day at home ... if they wanted to paint bloody pictures they'd find the time, don't worry.

GILLIAN. That's what you know. That's all you think.

WARREN. Cor blimey ... bored out of their minds, middle-class women.

SAUNDERS. Look at the rich, well-to-do women in the nineteenth century.

WARREN. Tell me they haven't had the opportunity or the time ...

SAUNDERS. As for the men ...

WARREN. Work their bollocks off feeding a bloody family, *then* come home and create a work of art ... you don't know when you're well off.

BRENDA. Piss off.

WARREN. You piss off.

CATHERINE. You piss off.

WARREN. And *you* piss off.

ALLOTT. Discussions of this sort invariably serve a useful function, clarifying the issues, setting them, if anything, in a wider context, removing the edge of personal, not to say sexual, vindictiveness ...

WARREN (*to* BRENDA). Get this up your nose you'd piss off all right.

BRENDA. Get this up somewhere else and you'd piss off all right.

ALLOTT. The education of the working class of course is still something of an anomaly.

WARREN (*to* BRENDA). Bollocks!

BRENDA. Bollocks.

WARREN. You haven't got no bollocks.

BRENDA. Neither have you!

(*Laughter from the girls.*)

ALLOTT. You could say that women have never had the *consciousness* to become artists—there are exceptions, but I mean as a general rule.

WARREN. Yeh, but, sir ...

SAUNDERS. I mean, don't you think that it would be extra-ordinary, Mr Allott, that something that has been denied women for so long should have taken all this time to emerge—I mean, their natural but frustrated capacity to be great thinkers, great composers, great artists, great poets ... great originators of thought and feeling? It seems humanly impossible that if this is an intrinsic part of the female temperament it should never have shown itself in any of these forms.

CATHERINE. Yeh ... but that's the point, i'n it? In women it's been made *unnatural*.

WARREN. Piss off.

CATHERINE. You piss off!

BRENDA. Whose side are you on, sir?

ALLOTT. Nobody's. That's to say, I'm accepting that any-thing is possible, but that for now, at this minute, Stella is standing there, in all her pristine glory ...

STELLA. I've got pins and needles.

ALLOTT. Whether women have been the object—or even the subject—of men's abuse, she is—and I insist that you still see her as—a human being. And it's as a human being you'll draw her, and it's as a human being you'll record your impressions of her ... insufferable to look at as some of those impressions well may be.

STELLA. Can I have a rest?

ALLOTT. No.

GILLIAN. Sir!

ALLOTT. She's always trying to get round me.

CATHERINE. Sir!

ALLOTT. If she'd really got pins and needles she'd have collapsed already. Can you feel a draught?

STELLA. No.

ALLOTT. Right, then.

MATHEWS (*entering*). Those bogs want cleaning out.
     (*Laughter.*)

GILLIAN. After you've been in, especially.

MATHEWS. *Afore* I went in ... That caretaker never goes in there. Sweeps to the bloody door then stops.

WARREN. What are you, Mathews, man or woman?

MATHEWS. If you've two minutes to step outside I'll show you.

WARREN. I mean in the political contest between the sexes, Bryan. Are you a man or are you a woman?

MATHEWS. I'm a woman. I'm on the woman's side in everything.

MOONEY. Front and back, an' all: it makes no difference to Mathews.

MATHEWS (*makes a fist*). You'll get this under your fucking nose.

BRENDA. How did your medicine work, then? Long and easy?

MATHEWS. And up yours ... I'm not above using this, you know.

WARREN. But slowly. Each evening, tha knows, afore he goes to bed.

(*Laughter from the girls.*)

MATHEWS. Piss off.

CATHERINE, GILLIAN *and* BRENDA (*together*). *Piss off!* (*They laugh.*)

ALLOTT. Coffee time, nearly. (*Examines his watch: winds it.*)

BRENDA. Aren't you going to do any drawing, sir?

ALLOTT. I might ... I might. (*Examines watch again.*) This time of the day the mind unfolds ... my time of life, however, Brenda, inspiration often falters.

CATHERINE. What about us, then, sir?

ALLOTT. I was coming to you, Catherine, as a matter of fact ... These invisible compositions ... You look (*indicates* STELLA.) ... Examine ... Set down ... But I'm damned if I can find a mark.

CATHERINE. There, sir.

ALLOTT. Where ...?

CATHERINE. Head ... arms ... legs ... feet.

ALLOTT. What's that?

CATHERINE. Her head, sir.

ALLOTT. It's a piece of fluff. (*Brushes it off with his hand.*) No it's not.

CATHERINE. It's her head, sir.

ALLOTT. What's this?

CATHERINE. Her breast, sir.

WARREN, MATHEWS *and* MOONEY (*together*). *Ooooh!*

ALLOTT. Where's the other one?

WARREN. She hasn't got one.

(*Laughter.*)

CATHERINE. I haven't done it, sir.

ALLOTT. There are two of these objects ... perhaps you

37

haven't noticed. And good grief. This other bit of fluff ...

CATHERINE. I was pin-pointing the principal masses, sir.

ALLOTT. You've been stabbing them to death. Just look at this.

(MATHEWS, *rising, has leaned over to look.*)

MATHEWS. One tit, one cunt: that's all she's got.

ALLOTT (*straightens: surveys* MATHEWS *for a moment. Then:*) I know your personality hasn't a great deal to recommend it, Mathews; but what little charm it does possess is scarcely enhanced by a remark like that ... If you could just concentrate on the job in hand.

WARREN. He hasn't got it in hand, sir; that's his trouble.

ALLOTT. The object, Mathews. The thing you see before you ... I take it that's your latest design for a coal-mine, Warren.

WARREN. Sir?

ALLOTT. Is there a human being lying somewhere under that?

WARREN. It's very difficult to concentrate here, sir.

ALLOTT. Michelangelo lay on his back all day to paint the Sistine ceiling ... he drew on his inner resources, Warren ...brought them up from deep inside.

(MATHEWS *belches.*)

Unaided, even, by patent laxative. (*Returns to* CATHERINE.) The problem, Catherine ... isn't to pin-point ... nor even to isolate ... it's to incorporate everything that is happening out there into a single homogeneous whole.

CATHERINE (*gazing at* STELLA). There's nothing happening, sir.

ALLOTT. There's a great deal happening ... Not in any obvious way ... nevertheless several momentous events are actually taking place out there ... subtly, quietly, not overtly ... but in the way that artistic events *do* take

38

place ... in the great reaches of the mind ... the way the leg, for instance, articulates with the hip, the shoulders with the thorax; the way the feet display the weight ... the hands subtended at the end of either arm ... these are the wonders of creation, Catherine ... Is your pen absolutely full? (*Has taken it to indicate the parts of the drawing to her: no mark. Shakes it down violently.*)

CATHERINE. Sir: you've blotted!

ALLOTT. Blots are indicative of industry, Catherine. Of energy. Passion. Draw round it. (*Rises, handing the pen to her.*)

WARREN. Could make it into your pubic, Cathy.

CATHERINE. Piss off.

WARREN. You piss off as well.

CARTER (*entering with cup and saucer*). Coffee up, sir.

ALLOTT. Not before time.

BRENDA. Rest, sir?

ALLOTT. The model is there, Brenda, for your edification. She's not a motif. Your glances in her direction—few and far between—are not to reassure yourself she's still in the room. She is there to be examined ... If only at a distance, Carter.

(STELLA *has whispered to* CARTER, '*Any for me?*'; *he's gone nearer to answer.*)

ALLOTT. ... If only at a distance, Carter.

CARTER. I didn't say anything, sir.

ALLOTT. Coffee cold?

CARTER. No, sir. It's just been made.

ALLOTT. I don't want to find anything in the saucer.

CARTER. No, sir.

ALLOTT. Hold it straight. (*To* MATHEWS) I'm not sure what comment I can make on Mathews' ... An advertisement, perhaps, for rubber tyres ... (*Twists his head.*) Or the effect of too much alcohol on the human brain ... (*Twists his head again.*) Burnt porridge, emerging through a Scotch mist ... at three, perhaps three thirty of a winter's morn ...

MATHEWS. I've not had time to get started, sir.

ALLOTT. That's what I mean ... The whole process, Mathews, has not begun: mass before beauty, excrescence before edification ... salaciousness before refinement ... Has anyone here seen Mr Philips?

BRENDA. No, sir.

GILLIAN. No, sir.

WARREN. No, sir.

MATHEWS. Got something on, then, have you?

ALLOTT. What?

(MATHEWS *makes the sound of a galloping horse, clicking his tongue against his teeth—and holding a pair of invisible reins, urgently, in his hands.*)

You still taking that medicine, Mathews?

MATHEWS. No, sir.

ALLOTT. Better get downstairs ... and take another dose. *Rest!*
(*Laughter: scramble for the door.*
STELLA *descends, stretching.*)

BRENDA. How long we got, sir?

ALLOTT. As long as I tell you.

WARREN. Watch it, Stella. (*Grapples with her.*)

STELLA. Get off, you filthy-minded beast.

(MATHEWS *blows raspberry: they all go, but for* SAUNDERS: *after getting up slowly, even reluctantly, he wanders round the drawings, examining.*)

ALLOTT. Going for a cup of tea, Samuel?

SAUNDERS. Yes, sir ... (*Casual*) Stella? You going?

STELLA. I'll be along in a minute, love ... My back ... Can you see anything on it? (*Turns it to* ALLOTT.)

ALLOTT. Here?

STELLA. No ...

ALLOTT. Here?

STELLA. Here ...

ALLOTT. What sort of thing?

STELLA. Knocked it ... when I got up it was terribly stiff ...
  I'll be along in a jiffy, Sammy.

SAUNDERS (*who's been waiting*). Oh ... all right. (*Glances at
  her: goes.*)

STELLA. Been measuring me again.

ALLOTT. Who?

STELLA. Sammy ... Look at all these plumb-lines ... Anybody'd think he was going to reconstruct me ... build me
  in concrete somewhere else.

ALLOTT. Your statistics are of immeasurable significance to
  him, Stella ... I can't see anything at all.

STELLA. You coming, are you? (*Puts on her dressing-gown.*)
    (CATHERINE *has come back in.*)

ALLOTT. No, no. I'll drink it here.

STELLA. See you. (*Goes.*)
    (CATHERINE *has gone to throne, sat down with her straw
    bag: gets out flask, sandwiches: pours tea.*
    ALLOTT *watches her. Then:*)

ALLOTT. Cucumber?

CATHERINE. Lettuce.

ALLOTT. Looks just like cucumber from over here.

CATHERINE. Lettuce.

ALLOTT. Don't you eat anything else?

CATHERINE. Haven't got time.

ALLOTT. My wife was coming up today.

CATHERINE. Is she, sir? What for?

ALLOTT. We've been separated, you know, for some
  considerable time. She's coming, I suspect, to give me
  news of a very significant nature ... or, in the terminology
  of the employment exchange, my cards.

CATHERINE. Oh, I'm sorry, sir.

ALLOTT. One of those things. The artist, after all, has no real life outside his work. Whenever he attempts it, the results, Catherine, leave—to say the very least of it—a great deal to be desired ... Refreshing.

CATHERINE. Yes, sir?

ALLOTT. Cucumber ... Don't you find it refreshing?

CATHERINE. Have one, sir, if you want.

ALLOTT. No. No ... I couldn't eat a thing.

CATHERINE. What sort of pictures do you paint, sir?

ALLOTT. I don't.

CATHERINE. Do you do sculpture, then?

ALLOTT. No. (*Shakes his head.*)

CATHERINE. What do you do, then, sir?

ALLOTT. It's my opinion that painting and sculpture, and all the traditional forms of expression in the plastic arts, have had their day, Catherine ... It's my opinion that the artist has been driven back—or driven on, to look at it in a positive way—to creating his works, as it were, in public.

CATHERINE. In public, sir?

ALLOTT. Just as Courbet or Modigliani, or the great Dutch Masters ... created their work out of everyday things, so the contemporary artist creates his work out of the experience—the events as well as the objects—with which he's surrounded in his day to day existence ... for instance, our meeting here today ... the feelings and intuitions expressed by all of us inside this room ... are in effect the creation—the re-creation—of the artist ... to the extent that they are controlled, manipulated, postulated, processed, defined, sifted, *re*fined ...

CATHERINE. Who by, sir?

ALLOTT. Well, for want a better word—by me.

(*Pause.*)

CATHERINE. Oh.

42

FOLEY (*entering*). Has somebody been bloody well smoking
in here?

    (FOLEY *is a bluff, red-faced man, an embryonic wrestler
in physique: about fifty to fifty-five.*)

ALLOTT (*standing immediately*). No.

FOLEY (*gazing round. Then:*) Who?

CATHERINE (*rising abruptly*). Catherine, sir.

FOLEY. Pipe tobacco ... they can't even be honest about it
and smoke a cigarette ... Think it'll get wafted up with
my own ... Think, you know, that a smoker can't smell
his own tobacco. I'm different in that respect ... Who?

CATHERINE. Catherine, sir.

FOLEY. What?

CATHERINE. Smith, sir.

FOLEY. Any relation to Walter Smith?

CATHERINE. No, sir.

FOLEY. Walter Smith's a very fine window cleaner. Cleans
my windows a treat. Where's everybody gone?

ALLOTT. Rest.

FOLEY. What's this? (WARREN'*s drawing.*)

ALLOTT. He's breaking it down, I believe ... into its individual
masses.

FOLEY. Crushing it to bloody death, it seems to me. (*Turns
the drawing upside down.*) The Black Hole of Calcutta ...
See it? ... All those figures? ... And that man trying to
claw his way towards the light ...

ALLOTT. Yes.

FOLEY. I should suggest he starts on it upside down.

ALLOTT. Yes.

FOLEY. What's this ...? (*Peers closely at* CATHERINE'*s.*)

ALLOTT. That's Catherine's, as a matter of fact.

FOLEY. Sat here all morning doing nowt, then.

ALLOTT. There are one or two marks ... indicative of the
principal masses.

43

FOLEY. T'ony thing I can see is a bloody blot ... Doesn't take long to draw a blot ... This the pen you use, then, is it? ... You don't want to use ought automatic when you turn to art ... automatic pens are out ... plastic paraphernalia that no artist of any note has any time for ... Sithee (*To* ALLOTT): when you set a pose, you want to set a teaser ... summat'll stretch em out ... arm up here ... leg out ... hip thrust in opposite direction (*Shows him.*) ... All this straight up and down nonsense, I reckon nowt to that ... The model doesn't smoke, then, does she?

ALLOTT. I'm not sure.

FOLEY (*looks behind screen*). Where's her undies?

ALLOTT. She changes in the ladies ... warmer.

FOLEY. No relation to Gordon Smith?

CATHERINE. No, sir.

FOLEY. Seen Philips, have you? (*Going.*)

ALLOTT. I was looking for him myself.

FOLEY. Think on: arm up, leg out. Get summat classical, tha knows. (*Goes.*)

    (CATHERINE *sighs. Sits down.*

    ALLOTT *sits too, after a moment.*)

CATHERINE. I didn't see you doing much controlling there, sir.

ALLOTT. I wouldn't agree with you entirely, Catherine ... Silence can guide, you know, as well as absorb.

CATHERINE. I don't think anyone guides Mr Foley.

ALLOTT. There are certain ungovernables in life, but even they can be incorporated into a general pattern—into a single, coherent whole ... other things, of course, don't have to be guided.

CATHERINE. Such as, sir?

ALLOTT. Natural impulses. Feeling creates its own form, form its own feeling.

CATHERINE. I'm not sure what you mean there, sir.

ALLOTT. Who can distinguish between the feeling, for instance, that informs a shape, and the shape itself? The one is a natural concomitant of the other ... indistinguishable. Inseparable.

(*Waits.*)

Then again, in personal feelings who's to say that what one feels for an individual can ever be separated from how they look, or are, or, indeed, as the phrase goes, have their being? I have my feelings about you, Catherine, and I associate them, irretrievably, with your appearance — how you walk, and speak ... is that your hat?

CATHERINE. I brought it this morning to show to Brenda.

ALLOTT. It's very becoming ...

(CATHERINE *puts it on, unselfconscious.*

ALLOTT *watches.*)

Really ...

CATHERINE. Do you like it?

ALLOTT. It's very beautiful ...

(CATHERINE *turns her head.*)

What could be simpler ...

I really think ... well. It's very charming.

(*Pause.*

WARREN *puts his head round the screen from the door.*)

WARREN. Foley's looking for a smoker ... In the women's bogs. Asked me if there was anyone I knew who smoked a pipe.

CATHERINE. He does.

WARREN. 'You, sir.' That's what I said. *He* said: 'None of your bloody cheek, Carter, or I'll clip you round the head.' I said, 'My name's Warren, sir.' He said, 'Well, I'll clip Warren round the head,' and added, after a moment's reflection, *threateningly*, 'You can tell him that from me.' (*To* CATHERINE) Was Saunders crying?

CATHERINE. Course he was ...

WARREN. Poorly, is he?

CATHERINE. He's in love with Stella.

WARREN. Can't be.

CATHERINE. Can't see why not.

ALLOTT. Artists have frequently been known to fall in love with the subject of their art.

WARREN. Not Saunders. He can't look at a tit without getting out a ruler.

ALLOTT. Perhaps it's the wrong instrument, but the instinct, I'm sure, is still the same.

WARREN. Who'd have believed it?

CATHERINE. I'll go and put my hat in the locker. It might get damaged up here.

WARREN. Might get nicked. (*Gesturing off.*)

CATHERINE. The women you can trust here, Warren. (*Goes.*)

    (WARREN *wanders aimlessly round the drawings. Then:*)

WARREN. You go in for all this art, then, sir?

ALLOTT. It's a job ...

WARREN. Doesn't seem real, somehow.

ALLOTT. We all sail, to some extent, under false colours, Warren ... I mean, you may not see yourself as an artist ... I may not see myself as a teacher ... No one of any consequence paints the human figure, for instance, any more ... it's not even a discipline because, if you presented me with a straight line and told me that's what you saw — under the absurd licence of modern illusionism — I'd have to accept it. Stella earns her living; I earn my living ... you earn your living — a mere pittance, I agree — one of the world's exploited ... but between us, we convene ... celebrate ... initiate ... an event, which, for me, is the very antithesis of what *you* term reality ... namely we embody, synthesize, evoke, a work, which, whether we are aware of it or not, is taking place around us ... (*Indicates* SAUNDERS' *entrance.*) all the time.

46

(WARREN *watches* SAUNDERS, *who makes no gesture to them: he crosses to the throne, sits there, on the edge, away from them. Then:*)

WARREN. All right, Sammy?

SAUNDERS. Yeh.

WARREN (*looking at* SAUNDERS' *drawing*). Not got much done for a morning.

SAUNDERS. No.

WARREN. Still ... Plenty of time yet, Sam.

SAUNDERS. Yeh.

(CARTER *enters: eyes on* SAUNDERS: *evidently been following him outside. He's followed in by* MATHEWS, *eyes on* SAUNDERS *too.*)

CARTER. How's Sammy?

SAUNDERS. All right.

MATHEWS. Cleared up, has it?

SAUNDERS. What?

MATHEWS. Eye ...

SAUNDERS. Yeh.

MATHEWS. Lot o' dust ... (*Wafts round.*) ... can see it circling ... (*Gazes up, following it with finger.*) Ooh! (*Clutches his eye.*)

WARREN. What's all this?

CARTER. Tell you later.

MATHEWS (*to* WARREN). S-a-m invited Stella out tonight.

WARREN. What's Stella say?

MATHEWS *and* CARTER (*together*). Piss off! (*They laugh.*)

(SAUNDERS *gets up: finds nowhere to go: goes to donkey: strips sheet of paper from his board. Sits.*)

WARREN. Mr Foley's been looking for a pipe-smoker, Sammy.

SAUNDERS. Has he?

WARREN. Got his suspicions.

MATHEWS. Came out of the women's bog.

CARTER. Dirty bugger ...

MATHEWS. Dirty sod!

WARREN. She was only an artist's daughter ...

MATHEWS. But she knew where to draw the line.

(*Laughter.*)

CARTER. Going, sir?

(ALLOTT *has made a move for the door.*)

ALLOTT. Yes ... I shan't be a moment ... Paper ... Pen ...
(*Feels in his pockets.*) Ah, yes. Here we are. (*Goes.*)

CARTER. Diarrhoea!

WARREN. Constipation!

MATHEWS. Poetry coming on!

(*They laugh.*)

WARREN. Why's he teach in this pissed-off dump?

SAUNDERS. Van Gogh couldn't even get a job.

MATHEWS. Who's Van Gogh?

(*Laughter.*)

SAUNDERS. Don't judge people by appearances; that's all,
Warren.

CARTER. That's your considered opinion is it, Sammy?

SAUNDERS. It's not considered. It's just a simple fact of life.

MATHEWS. You know a lot about life then, Sammy.

SAUNDERS. I don't know much at all, as a matter of fact. I
know something about Mr Allott, though.

CARTER. What?

SAUNDERS. That he's sincere in his beliefs.

WARREN. Is he?

(SAUNDERS *doesn't answer.*)

MATHEWS. What beliefs are those, when they're all at
home?

SAUNDERS. Perhaps there isn't a role left for the artist ...
perhaps, in an egalitarian society – so-called – an artist is a
liability ... after all, he's an individual: he tells you by his
gift alone that all people can't be equal ... why should one

person have a beautiful voice if we can't all have it ...? That's what it's coming to ... That's an opinion, however, not a fact of life.

CARTER. Why go on measuring up all these beautiful women, Sammy?

SAUNDERS. There's something dispassionate in human nature ... that's what I think ... something really dispassionate that nothing—no amount of pernicious and cruel experience—can ever destroy. That's what I believe in ... I think a time will come when people will be interested in what was dispassionate at a time like this ... when everything was dictated to by so much fashion ... by fashion and techniques.

WARREN. You draw like a machine: what you worrying about?

SAUNDERS. I use a bit of string, and a stone. If I can't measure what I see how can I relate it?

WARREN. Silly prick.

CARTER. He talks like Allott.

WARREN. He looks like Allott.

MATHEWS. He smells like Allott.

CARTER, WARREN *and* MATHEWS (*together*). *He is Allott!* (*They laugh.*)

(BRENDA *comes in.*)

BRENDA. Have we started?

CARTER. Not yet, my darling. (*Embraces her.*)

BRENDA. Get off ... (*Stays in his embrace, however.*) That coffee does terrible things to your stomach.

MATHEWS. Come a bit closer and I might do something better.

BRENDA. Piss off. (*Sways with* CARTER *in embrace.*)

WARREN. I don't think women should swear, as a matter of fact.

MATHEWS. Neither do I.

49

BRENDA. Why not?

WARREN. I'll tell you why ... I've never heard *one* who can do it with conviction.

BRENDA. Fuck off.

WARREN (*to* CARTER). There's a first time, you see, for everything.

(CATHERINE *enters, gasping.*)

CATHERINE. Have we started?

BRENDA. No, love. (*Kissing* CARTER, *in whose arms she still sways.*)

CATHERINE. Once up and down the stairs ... (*Collapses on donkey.*)

WARREN. Why d'you do it, Catherine?

CATHERINE. Get varicose veins, you know, with sitting.

MATHEWS. I could give you all the exercise you want.

CATHERINE. So I've heard.

WARREN. Follows you up and down, he does.

CARTER. Stairs ...

WARREN. Likes the colour of your knickers.

CATHERINE. That's as close as he'll ever get.

MATHEWS. I think women ought to wear trousers, as a matter of fact.

BRENDA. Why?

(CARTER *has already released her.*)

MATHEWS. Look silly wearing skirts. Men don't show off their underwear, do they?

BRENDA. Not your dirty, filthy, bloody stuff.

MATHEWS. Piss off.

WARREN. Get your hand in easier, Bryan. (*Gropes* BRENDA.)

MATHEWS. Yeh ... Hadn't thought of that!

BRENDA. Piss off.

WARREN. Piss off yourself ... (*Raspberry.*)

(MATHEWS *joins* WARREN *with* BRENDA: *they fight.*)
PHILIPS *enters.*)

PHILIPS (*briskly*). Morning, boys ... Mr Allott about, then,
is he? ... Morning, ladies.

(PHILIPS *is a small, dapper, military figure, stiff, between
forty and fifty: he bows to the two girls as the fighting
subsides.*)

WARREN. He's popped out for a moment, Mr Philips.

PHILIPS. By go, rest time, is it?

CARTER. Yes, sir.

MATHEWS. Was there any message in particular you wanted
passing on, sir?

PHILIPS (*crossing to throne and heaters*). Lovely and warm in
here ... Warmest room in the building.

WARREN. We're about to start any minute, sir.

PHILIPS. I'll hang on. I'll hang on. (*Warms his hands at the
heater.*) By God: tempted to become a model, you know,
myself.

CARTER. Is it true at one time, sir, you were an amateur
boxer? (*Glancing at the others.*)

PHILIPS. That's quite correct.

CARTER. Lightweight, sir?

PHILIPS. Oh, one of the lightweight categories, you can be
sure of that ...

WARREN. Still in good shape, sir.

PHILIPS. I could give a round or two to some of these
youngsters nowadays ... Two days of roadwork and they
want to turn professional ... By God, some of the best
boxers of the day, you know, were amateur ... never
stepped inside a professional ring. Knew what the business
was all about and had their priorities in the proper order.
The moment sport and money mix, the former—you can
take it from me—goes out of the window.

STELLA (*entering*). Time is it?

PHILIPS. My God, and come out fighting! (*Dances forward,
fists ready: laughs.*)

STELLA. Oh, Mr Philips ...

PHILIPS. Up on your throne, young lady. Give it all you've got ... Come on, come on, there. Mr Allott can't be far away, I can tell you that.

> (*They go slowly to their respective easels and donkeys.*
>
> SAUNDERS, *who has been sharpening his pencil since his last dialogue, has attached a fresh sheet of paper to his drawing-board.*
>
> STELLA *mounts the platform.*)

Few masterpieces I can see already on the way ... Might turn that into a lithograph, Carter ... one or two nice textures there ...

CARTER. That's Warren's.

PHILIPS. All true art is impersonal. Who said that?

MATHEWS. Mr Allott, sir.

PHILIPS (*pause. Then:*) That's quite correct.

STELLA. Well ... Are you ready?

WARREN. Ready.

MATHEWS. Ready.

CARTER. Ready.

STELLA. For *drawing.*

WARREN. Mr Philips is dying for a look ...

PHILIPS. Oh, I've seen plenty of models in my time, I can tell you that ... Those of us in the Design Department aren't that far removed from life ... Now, what's the pose ... ? Chalk marks all correct?

> (PHILIPS *stands by the throne.*
>
> STELLA *removes her robe.*
>
> PHILIPS *gazes at her:*)

Left ... more left ... (*Glances at one of the drawings.*) Right hand ... That's correct ... (*Looks round.*) Everyone satisfied?

WARREN. If you are, sir.

PHILIPS. Oh, I'm satisfied ... I'm satisfied well enough ... Catherine, my dear?

CATHERINE. Yes, sir.

PHILIPS. Brenda?

BRENDA. Yes, sir.

> (*They all begin.*
>
> *They work in silence: gradually, one by one, heads turn and gaze at* SAUNDERS *who, solemnly, has begun his measuring out and his careful drawing. After a while the whole room's attention is on him, even finally* STELLA *herself, who, without moving her body, turns her head and looks.*
>
> SAUNDERS, *aware of their gaze, looks up.*
>
> PHILIPS, *who has been inspecting the girls' drawings from behind their backs, looks up too.*)

PHILIPS. Is anything the matter?

WARREN. No, sir.

MATHEWS. No, sir.

CARTER. No, sir.

BRENDA. No, sir.

CATHERINE. No, sir.

PHILIPS. Well, then ... Get on with it.

> (*They begin again. After a while the heads begin to turn again: finally they all gaze at* SAUNDERS.
>
> SAUNDERS, *drawing, becomes aware of their fresh scrutiny. After a moment's hesitation he gets up: takes up his plumb-line, his various pieces, his board, his paper.*
>
> GILLIAN *and* MOONEY *come in as* SAUNDERS *leaves. He brushes past them, goes.*)

MOONEY. What's up with Sammy, then?

CARTER. Love-sick.

WARREN. Silly pillock.

> (MATHEWS *blows raspberry.*)

GILLIAN. Hello, Mr Philips.

MOONEY. Filling in ...?

PHILIPS. Temporary absence of Mr Allott ... And which is your drawing, my dear?

GILLIAN. This one.

PHILIPS. Delicate ... very delicate. (*Examines it, then indicates* STELLA.) You'll notice ... (*Crosses to* STELLA.) the thigh ... (*Runs his hand along it.*) is relaxed when the weight is on the other foot ... it's suspended from the pelvis ... here ... at a lower point than where—because it's taking the weight—it's *inserted* on the other side ... (*Demonstrates with both hands.*)

GILLIAN. Yes.

PHILIPS. The hips, therefore, represent something of an acute angle, subtended from the horizontal.

WARREN. He's not going to grope her, is he?

PHILIPS. Have I made it clear?

GILLIAN. Yes, sir.

> (PHILIPS *moves back to the drawings: walks around the rear of the students: leans over one or two boys.*)

PHILIPS (*to* CARTER). More ... That's better ... (*Points it out on the paper. Moves on. To* WARREN) Clearer ... clearer ... A good clean line ... (*To* MATHEWS, *after a quick perusal and passing on*) That's coming on ...

> (*Work in silence for a while.*
>
> *In the silence* ALLOTT *enters: unnatural: looks round. Pause. Then:*)

ALLOTT. Where's Saunders, then?

CARTER. Love-sick, sir.

PHILIPS. Temporarily absented ... One or two nice effects ... (*Indicates students' work.*)

ALLOTT. Blue Moon came up at Kempton.

PHILIPS. Do you want it in tens or fives?

ALLOTT. It always feels much better in shillings. (*Holds out his hand.*)

> (PHILIPS *sorts coins: hands them over.*)

Looked for you all over this morning.

PHILIPS. Dear boy: I've only just arrived.

ALLOTT. You don't understand, Philips. This is the first time I've ever won.

PHILIPS. Incredible, old boy ... No, no. Really. (*Sorts last coin: hands it over.*)

ALLOTT (*gazing up*). Somewhere, in that indefinable miasma we call life, there's some creature looking down ... 'Allott,' it said. 'Allott ... Let Allott win the four-fifteen.'

PHILIPS. Nearly the three o'clock as well.

ALLOTT. That was a different matter entirely.

PHILIPS. I said go for a place, old boy.

ALLOTT. I just felt that fate had bigger things in store.

PHILIPS. It had. It had.

ALLOTT (*gazes at the coins in his hand. Then:*) I'd almost given up hope, Philips.

PHILIPS. Don't give up hope, old boy ... After all, what're we in this business for ... No. This. (*Indicates the model, room.*)

ALLOTT. Ah ... Yes.

PHILIPS. Posterity, old son. If they don't see it now they'll see it later. We're building up an enormous credit ... (*Gestures aimlessly overhead.*) somewhere ... You with your ... events ... me with my designs ... book-jackets, posters ... Letraset ... singular embodiments of the age we live in.

ALLOTT. Sold anything lately?

PHILIPS (*shakes his head*). ... You?

ALLOTT. How do you sell an event that no one will admit is taking place?

PHILIPS. Have to go back to painting, old boy.

ALLOTT. I know when I'm licked, Philips. It's all or nothing ... the avant-garde or bust.

PHILIPS. Old boy ...

ALLOTT. It's not important.

PHILIPS. Don't give up ... that's the message ... that's the message that comes down to us from Rembrandt ... from Cézanne ... from all that countless host who sank their existences in art ...

ALLOTT. Don't you get the feeling at times that it's a substitute for living?

PHILIPS. This *is* life ... Dear boy ... just look around you ... the youth of today ... the human body (*Indicates* STELLA.) ... what more could one desire?

ALLOTT. You're right.

PHILIPS. How much do you want on?

ALLOTT. I haven't looked at a paper yet ... I haven't got over the shock of this one ... I even told my wife ... on the phone, you know ... we've been separated now for several months ... '25p?' she said. 'You're going crazy.' And the fact of the matter is, at times, I really think I am.

PHILIPS. Baudelaire ... Dostoevsky ... Nietzsche ... you have to bear them all in mind ... men who teetered on the very brink of human existence and had the privilege — the temerity, even — to gaze right over the edge ...

ALLOTT. I've gazed over the edge, Philips, long enough ... it's the staying there that worries me ... I'm beginning to think I'll never get back ... How does one live as a revolutionary, Philips, when no one admits there's a revolution there?

PHILIPS. Prophet in his own country, old boy ... Think of Christ.

ALLOTT. I think of nothing else ... I'm even beginning to think, Philips, that it's not my duty to resurrect mankind.

PHILIPS. Stranger things have happened, boy ... Lucky Horseshoe, two-fifteen ... obvious choice ... But then Blue Moon stuck out a mile.

ALLOTT. How much?

PHILIPS. Can get you eight to one, old boy.

ALLOTT (*counting his money*). 10p ... leaves me with 15.

PHILIPS. That's the spirit ... (*Takes the money.*) Anything worth doing ... (*To* CATHERINE *as he leaves*) Firmer! Firmer! ... (*To* ALLOTT) Commit yourself: that's all it means. (*Goes.*)

(ALLOTT *stands there for a while; gazes before him, abstracted. Then:*)

ALLOTT. All right ... Everyone?

BRENDA. Yes, sir.

CATHERINE. Yes, sir.

GILLIAN. Yes, sir.

MOONEY. Yes, sir.

WARREN. Yes, sir.

ALLOTT. Good ...

MATHEWS. *Yes, sir!*

ALLOTT. Good ... good. That's the spirit ... Labor Ipse Voluptas Est.

WARREN. Rest, sir?

ALLOTT. No, no ... Just carry on.

(*Fade.*)

# ACT TWO

## Scene 1

*Stage empty. Light faint.*

ABERCROMBIE *comes on, dressed in sweater, scarf, plimsolls, shorts. Carries a racquet.*

*Silence.*

ABERCROMBIE. I say ... (*Returns to screen: a moment later lights come on. Comes back.*) Anyone for squash?

(*Groan from behind model's screen.*

*Goes to screen: looks behind.*)

I'm terribly sorry ...

STELLA (*heard, stretching*). Ooooh ... !

ABERCROMBIE. Fancy a knock-up?

STELLA (*heard*). No thanks.

ABERCROMBIE. Looks like thunder. (*Indicates off.*)

STELLA (*emerging in dressing-gown*). I was sleeping ... (*Stretches.*) It's so much quieter lying in here,

ABERCROMBIE (*ducking down and gazing up*). Or snow ...

STELLA. Play that often?

ABERCROMBIE. Lunch times ... winter mostly. Summer — tennis.

STELLA. Oh ... (*Stretches. Yawns.*) Make me feel so lazy ... Got a cigarette?

(ABERCROMBIE *takes cigarette packet from trouser-pocket.*)

Give you one back ... Left em in me knickers.

(ABERCROMBIE *lights her cigarette with a lighter.*)

Foley not around? (*Blows out smoke.*)

ABERCROMBIE. Doubt it.

STELLA. Been in his office have you?

ABERCROMBIE. Not very often.

STELLA. Seen his jars ...? *Bottles* ... Along the shelves ... Use them in chemistry labs, for acid.

ABERCROMBIE. Now you mention it.

STELLA. Full of urine.

ABERCROMBIE. What?

STELLA. Broke one, one day ... cleaners. Terrible pong ... His lavatory ... would you believe, is full of broken statues ... Venus de Milo in plaster-cast ... all sorts of rubbish he's collected.

ABERCROMBIE. Good God.

STELLA. Keeps his pee in bottles: anything artistic – down the lav.

ABERCROMBIE. Good lord.

STELLA. Suppose that's genius, really.

ABERCROMBIE. Yes ...

STELLA. Modern art.

(*Pause.*)

ABERCROMBIE. That's right. (*Looks around for* ALLOTT.)

STELLA. He was here not long ago ... Mr Allott ... Heard him singing.

ABERCROMBIE. Singing?

STELLA. He sings, you know, when he's on his own ... Didn't know I was here, you see.

ABERCROMBIE. Ah, yes.

STELLA. What you use? (*Indicates racquet.*)

ABERCROMBIE. A rubber ball.

STELLA. I've always been interested, you know, in sport ...

ABERCROMBIE. Ah, yes ...

STELLA. My own colour, that. (*Reveals her shoulder.*)

ABERCROMBIE. Good lord.

STELLA. I've a greasy skin. Just feel at that.

ABERCROMBIE. It's very soft.

STELLA. A woman should be soft.

ABERCROMBIE. You've got very nice legs, of course.

STELLA. They're not so bad ... woman my age. (*Shows him.*)

ABERCROMBIE. Don't know why you bother with that. (*Indicates dressing-gown.*)

STELLA. Can't sleep in me altogether. Not safe to in a place like this.

ABERCROMBIE. One or two custodians of morality about.

STELLA. Like who?

ABERCROMBIE. Me.

STELLA. Not from some of the tales I've heard.

ABERCROMBIE. Such as?

STELLA. Mr Abercrombie is a well-known character in some quarters of the town.

ABERCROMBIE. The tennis courts are the only place I frequent with any regularity ... and the squash courts, too, of course.

> (STELLA *turns back to the screen.*)

Room for two in there?

STELLA. There might.

ABERCROMBIE. Have a smoke, I think, myself ... Give it up ... (*Coughs.*) Chest ... Never persist for very long.

STELLA. Sit, mind you. And nothing else.

> (ABERCROMBIE *has gone behind the screen.*
> STELLA *follows.*
> After a moment* ALLOTT *enters: slow. Takes hat off: sits down on edge of throne in his coat.*)

STELLA (*heard*). Never ... (*Laughter.*)

ABERCROMBIE (*heard*). As God is my witness.

STELLA (*heard*). All over?

ABERCROMBIE (*heard*). That's what the genius said. (*Laughter, heard.*)

> (ALLOTT *glances up: no interest: sits with arms on his knees.*
> FOLEY *enters: stands there a moment, smoking pipe: takes it out.*)

FOLEY. Bloody place is like a mausoleum.

ALLOTT. Yes.

FOLEY. Lunch hour.

ALLOTT. Yes.

FOLEY. Chisel-marks on that wall out theer ... Bring them up, you know, from the sculpture room: safe-keeping in their lockers. What they do? Start taking the bloody place apart. (*Gazes round: finally looks up. Reads:*)

> 'Foley is never surely
> Going to keep us solely
> On potato crisps for long.'

Chalk.

ALLOTT. Yes.

FOLEY. Up yonder ...

ALLOTT (*looks*). Yes.

FOLEY. Know the author?

ALLOTT. No. (*Shakes his head.*)

    (*Pause.* FOLEY *looks round again. Pause.*)

FOLEY. Disillusioning place, is this.

ALLOTT. In what way?

FOLEY. Students of today ... two minutes with a bucket of plaster ... half a pot o' paint ... a bit o' wire ... turn out some conundrum on a piece of hardboard and think they've done a Mona Lisa. When you think this is where the Donatellos and the Verrocchios of the future are supposed to come from it begins to shake your faith.

    (*Sits down on the throne beside* ALLOTT.)

Ever think about life, then, do you?

ALLOTT (*hesitates for some considerable time. Then:*) No.

FOLEY. In my youth you thought of nothing else: life ... (*Gazes up. Pause.*) Infinity ...

    (*Pause. Abstracted. Then:*)

Altered the pose, then, have you?

ALLOTT. I thought I'd bear it in mind ... for a future occasion.

FOLEY. Classical, Allott. Classical. Every time. The distillation of history. The classical is the finest embodiment of the human spirit. That's what we're here to instil. A respect for the past and a clean and wholesome acceptance of the present ... Vegetarian?

ALLOTT (*looks up*). No.

FOLEY. Do you know what's involved in the killing of a cow?

ALLOTT (*hesitates. Then:*) No.

FOLEY. The dismemberment of a living body?

ALLOTT. No. (*Shakes his head.*)

FOLEY. I went to a butchery on one occasion ... I don't call it by any of these fancy names ... I went, ostensibly, to do some sketches – that's what I told the management – once there I found I couldn't draw a thing ... Blood there was. Everywhere ... intestines, bladders, stomachs, livers ... the appalling desecration of life ... the living reduced to an inanimate mass.

(*Pause.*)

Speak?

ALLOTT. No. (*Shakes his head.*)

FOLEY. I've never touched a piece of meat since then. Every time a piece of meat is presented to me at table ... (*Takes out penknife.*) Cut my thumb.

ALLOTT (*pause. Then:*) Isn't it very dangerous?

FOLEY. I disinfect the blade ... (*Shows him blade.*) Turns one or two stomachs, I can tell you that ... I use it occasionally, too, for sharpening pencils. (*Snaps blade to.*) Not in the dining-room, I thought, today.

ALLOTT. No.

FOLEY. A consequence of illogical eating is illogical art. All good art is based on a good digestion. It's what these let-it-happen boys have never understood. Here today and gone tomorrow. They think abstraction, you know, can take art across national frontiers. Fact of the

63

matter is, all the profoundest art is regional. It takes time for its universal principles to be revealed. For instance, who would have thought that a meticulous and obsessive interest in the Auvergne countryside would have made Cézanne one of the greatest—if not the greatest – painter of the present age. Draw a few rings, a few lines ... blocks of colour, and because it's immediately recognizable in Tokyo, Lisbon and New York, think it must be significant ... instant communication is the fallacy of the time. All these marvellous means for one human being to communicate with another—wireless, television, planes. What happens? Some terrible song-and-dance routine ... beyond that: æons of triviality perpetuating itself across the vast distances of inter-stellar space.

ALLOTT. I didn't eat because my wife has decided to divorce me, as a matter of fact.

FOLEY. Marriage for an artist is an anomaly in any case. When a man's life is illuminated by an inner vision, everything outside is pure distraction.

ALLOTT. That's her opinion exactly ... (*Gets up.*) She thinks— with my working here—I'm neither one thing nor another ... My creations – including, I would have thought, my marriage—invisible events which only I can see ...

FOLEY (*rising*). There's someone, you know, behind that screen. (*Goes over.*) Just look at this.

STELLA (*heard*). Hello, Mr Foley.

FOLEY. Not been smoking by any chance, then, have you?

ABERCROMBIE (*heard*). No, sir. (*Comes out stretching, glancing at* ALLOTT.) Fancy a shot or two, old man? (*Racquet.*)

ALLOTT. No, thanks.

FOLEY. Smell smoke, you know, a mile off. I've an extremely sensitive nose for smoke. If somebody lights up a cigarette a mile off I can smell it in a matter of seconds.

ALLOTT (*gazing up, reading*).

> 'Some talk of Alexander and some of Hercules,
>> But what of old Verrocchio and ancient Pericles?'

(FOLEY *looks up too, and* ABERCROMBIE.)

FOLEY. How they get up there beats me ... It takes somebody more sophisticated than a student to think up rhymes like that.

ALLOTT (*reading*).

>> 'Teachers love to make a bit:
>>> All students do is shovel ...'

FOLEY. It's not your casual two-minute composition that ... there's fifteen-minutes' worth of lettering on that wall.

ALLOTT (*reads, in a fresh direction*).

>> 'Allott is a parrot,
>> Foley is a scream:
>> Abercrombie's like a carrot,
>> And Philips's just a queen.'

FOLEY. Get the whitewash in here this evening. You can't turn your back on that. The Director of Education came in the other day. Know what was inscribed in the front doorway? 'Education is the opium of the middle classes.' My father was a cobbler, and, before that, his father was a blacksmith.

ABERCROMBIE. You've come a long way, Mr Foley.

FOLEY. I have ... I have ... I'll not have them forget it ... (*Sees* ABERCROMBIE *as if for the first time.*) You here for the Monte Carlo Rally, are you?

ABERCROMBIE. Squash.

FOLEY. There's no squash in this building, I can tell you that. Sport and art don't mix. What stimulates the brain stimulates the body: you don't need to go chasing balls to keep fit ... We'll have that removed before I go tonight. (*Going: to* ALLOTT) Classical. Classical ... It's the eternal, Allott, that really lasts. (*Goes.*)

(ALLOTT *sits down. He's still got on his coat. Pause.*
ABERCROMBIE *regards him for a moment. Then:*)

STELLA. I think I'll go for a pee. (*Goes.*)

ABERCROMBIE. True?

(ALLOTT *looks up.*)

Missis.

ALLOTT. My life has been a continual saga of good intentions,
Abercrombie ... I only became an artist because I thought
that way I'd be of least trouble to anybody else ... who's
ever heard of an artist who's a liability?

ABERCROMBIE. Fancy a game or two, old man?

ALLOTT. Recline here, I think ... Swot up on one or two
classical poses ... 'The Suicide's Revenge' ... 'Love in
Clover' ... 'The Disinterested Man's Delight'.

ABERCROMBIE. Changeable situation ... Might be back in
time for bed.

ALLOTT. Not mine, I'm afraid. I'm sure of that.

ABERCROMBIE. Sure about the ...? (*Swings racquet.*)

(ALLOTT *nods.*)

ABERCROMBIE. See you.

ALLOTT. See you.

(ABERCROMBIE *goes.*

ALLOTT, *after a while, gets up: walks slowly round the
stools. Finally sits down at one: gazes at the throne.
Pause.*

*After a little while* MATHEWS *comes in, whistling.*)

MATHEWS. Sir. (*Nods.*)

(ALLOTT *nods.*)

MATHEWS. Mind? (*Indicates donkey.*)

ALLOTT. Not really.

MATHEWS. Stella ...? (*Nods at screen.*)

(ALLOTT *shakes his head.*)

MATHEWS. Fancy a bit of that ... You know ... time to time.

Not above it when you catch her on her own. Other people around: screams blue murder.

(*Pause.*)

Seen Foley ...

ALLOTT. Yes.

MATHEWS. Tell you yesterday what happened?

ALLOTT. No ...

MATHEWS. Came in ... late ... School as quiet as death ... tip-toe up the stairs: look behind ... *entering* the hall below is a very large piece of ... can you guess?

(ALLOTT, *after some moments' hesitation, shakes his head.*)

MATHEWS. Coal ... (*Waits for* ALLOTT'*s reaction.*) Two hands clasped to this gigantic piece of coal ... big as a house ... Know who it was? ... Foley! ... head comes into view ... Looks this way ... looks that ... coal held out ... looks up. Sees me. Know what he does? ... Steps *backwards* ... Couldn't believe it. Ever so slowly. After a few seconds this gigantic lump of coal just disappears ... I go on up the stairs ... Mark time. Steps get fainter ... Two minutes later ... piece of coal comes back ... two hands ... Foley ... Tuck my head in ... Steps out across the hall ... Let him get half way ... Call: '*Mr Foley, have you got a minute?*' ... Should have seen it ... crash like thunder ... Look down ... bits of coal all over the hall ... Next thing: belting up the stairs and calling: '*Anybody smoking up here, then, is there?*' (*Laughs.*)

(ALLOTT *no reaction.*

*Pause.*)

Tell me he's a kleptomaniac.

ALLOTT. Is that so?

MATHEWS. Catch him one day.

ALLOTT. Sure to.

MATHEWS. Be in for the high-jump: can tell you that.

ALLOTT. There are plans, as a matter of fact, to replace this college with an Institute of Engineering ... the designs are quite advanced, I understand ... octagonal building with vertical lighting—no windows except in the roof—and a large gallery at one end for the mounting of exceptionally large pieces of machinery ... what we want, in a nutshell, but it'll be given over exclusively to engines.

(MATHEWS *has mounted the throne.*)

MATHEWS. Fancied modelling, you know, myself ... Do muscle exercises in the evening ... (*Poses.*) ... no threat of redundancy ... alus somebody to look at somebody else.

ALLOTT. Yes.

(*Pause. He gazes at* MATHEWS.)

If you stand there for a moment ... (*Takes out pad, pencil.*)

MATHEWS (*poses*). This do you?

ALLOTT. Anything that comes natural.

(MATHEWS *poses.*

ALLOTT *draws casually. Silence.*)

MATHEWS. Strip down if you like.

ALLOTT. I think this'll do perfectly ... you're posing very well.

MATHEWS. Think I'm loud-mouthed ... (*Gestures off.*) Them ... Fact is—do you mind me talking?—you act up to what people expect of you.

ALLOTT. How do you know what they expect?

MATHEWS. Feel it ...

ALLOTT. Suppose you're mistaken?

MATHEWS. Not here.

ALLOTT. Suppose really they'd been expecting someone different?

MATHEWS. How different?

ALLOTT. Sensitive ... intelligent ... (*Still drawing.*) perhaps even quietly mannered.

MATHEWS. My looks?

ALLOTT. Looks can be deceptive.

MATHEWS. Long-distance only ...

ALLOTT. Seen that wall?

MATHEWS. One o' your rhymes.

ALLOTT. Hardly.

MATHEWS. What?

ALLOTT. Not that tall.

MATHEWS (*reads*). 'O where has the significance of life gone to ...'

ALLOTT (*without looking up*). 'My mother said.'

MATHEWS. '... If it's not where we might expect it, it must be in some other place instead.'

ALLOTT. Moving.

MATHEWS. Oh ... Yeh. (*Adjusts his pose.*)

ALLOTT. That's better ... No. No. That's fine. (*Draws in silence for a while.*)

    (PHILIPS *comes in.*)

PHILIPS. Bet on ... Odds as mentioned ... (*Sees* MATHEWS.) Carter.

MATHEWS. Mathews.

PHILIPS. Mathews.

    (*Gazes at* MATHEWS *for some time.*)

MATHEWS (*finally, under* PHILIPS' *gaze*). Mind if I get down, sir?

ALLOTT. One more minute.

MATHEWS. Arms ache.

ALLOTT. Ten seconds.

MATHEWS. Harder than you think.

PHILIPS. When I was in the pink could stand, utterly immobile, for an hour and a half ... Reflex: a conditioned reflex. What's required, ironically enough, is to be utterly relaxed.

ALLOTT. Five.

PHILIPS. I've got the slip ... Lucky Horseshoe.

ALLOTT. I'll never need it.

PHILIPS. Odds had shortened before I left. Sevens. It'll be three to one by the time they reach the post.

ALLOTT. Two.

MATHEWS. I'm going dizzy.

ALLOTT. Hold it. Hold it.

> (MATHEWS, *after a strenuous effort to keep still, collapses.*
> ALLOTT *goes on drawing for a moment.*
> MATHEWS *sits moaning, massaging.*
> ALLOTT *finally looks up: looks about him. Then:*)

Take this off ... (*Coat: stands: removes it.*) Hang it. (*Feels in his pockets.*) Shan't be long. (*Goes.*)

MATHEWS. First time I've seen his drawing.

PHILIPS. One of the leading exponents of representational art in his youth, was Mr Allott ... You'd have to go back to Michelangelo to find a suitable comparison ...

> (MATHEWS *stoops over pad: peers closely.*)

MATHEWS. There's nothing there ...

PHILIPS. Now, of course ... an impresario ... purveyor of the invisible event ... so far ahead of his time you never see it.

MATHEWS. I've been posing there for half an hour!

PHILIPS. Longer, I'd imagine.

MATHEWS (*picks up pad: examines other pages. Reads finally:*)
> 'Oh, she was good all right in patches,
> She was good all right in bed:
> But where would it all have ended
> If I'd loved her like I said?'

PHILIPS. I really think that's private property, old boy.

MATHEWS (*reads*).
> 'Oh, we'll listen to the wireless
> And lie in bed till three;
> "Turn up the volume, lady."
> Oh, love is good to me.'
> (*Evades* PHILIPS' *effort to take the pad.*)

> 'Oh, he found love in valleys,
> In caves and crannies too;
> Fissures, where a lover
> Could find what lovers do.'

PHILIPS. I think, really, that belongs to me ... is in my custody ... my supervision.

MATHEWS (*reads*).

> 'He called her night and morning;
> He sat beside the phone:
> What's mine is yours, she told him:
> Oh, give a dog a bone!'

PHILIPS. I'm appealing to you, Mathews, as a member of the staff ... as a respected and somewhat elderly member of the staff ... lightweight champion of the northern counties and—for several months previous to that—of one of the more prominent of the southern counties as well.

MATHEWS (*reads*).

> 'He waited, how he waited;
> He waited for his love:
> She'd meant to get there early,
> But went back for her glove.'

PHILIPS. See here, Mathews ... That's private property.

MATHEWS. Here ... just look at this. (*Shows it to* PHILIPS.)

PHILIPS (*reads*). 'I shall kill Foley ... Foley is very poorly ...

> Foley is surely ...
> the person I shall hourly ...
> kill ...
> whenever poor old Allott gets the chance ...'

MATHEWS. 'Poor old Allott is the ...'

PHILIPS. 'Apotheosis ...'

MATHEWS. 'Poor old Allott is the ...'

PHILIPS. 'Amanuensis ...'

MATHEWS. 'Poor old Allott is the ...'

PHILIPS. 'Polarity ...'

MATHEWS. 'From which this world began ...'

PHILIPS. 'Poor old Al ...'

MATHEWS. 'Poor old Allott ...'

PHILIPS. 'Dirge on a forgotten planet ...'

MATHEWS. 'Allott is the palette ...'

PHILIPS. 'On which my sins began ...'

MATHEWS. 'First ...'

PHILIPS. 'He was a saviour ...'

MATHEWS. 'Secondly ...'

PHILIPS. 'A saint ...'

MATHEWS. 'Thirdly ...'

PHILIPS. 'Lost his chances ...'

MATHEWS. 'Fourthly ...'

PHILIPS. 'Learnt to paint.'

MATHEWS. 'Fifthly ...'

PHILIPS. 'Came to pieces ...'

MATHEWS. 'Sixthly ...'

PHILIPS. 'Showed his hand.'

MATHEWS. 'Seventhly ...'

PHILIPS. 'Set his creases ...'

MATHEWS. 'Eighthly ...'

PHILIPS. 'Joined the band.'

MATHEWS. 'Ninthly ...'

PHILIPS. 'Went to heaven ...'

MATHEWS. 'Tenthly ...'

PHILIPS. 'Rang the bell.'

MATHEWS. 'Eleventhly ...'

PHILIPS. 'Thought he'd better ...'

MATHEWS. 'Twelfthly ...'

ALLOTT (*having entered*). 'Go to hell' ... No, no, really, Philips ... Once started, carry on ...

PHILIPS. I was trying to get it from him. I was even — would you believe it — threatening him with physical violence.

MATHEWS. Private, sir. (*Hands it back.*) I was just looking at the drawing, sir.

ALLOTT. There isn't any drawing ... or, rather, the drawing was the drawing ... perhaps you weren't aware.

MATHEWS. No, sir.

(*Pause. Then:*)

I'll go and get my board, sir.

ALLOTT. Right.

(MATHEWS *hesitates: glances from one to the other: goes.*)

PHILIPS (*examines watch*). Better be getting back ... Proceedings start in seven minutes ... Six and a half to be exact ... Carter moved the platform slightly.

ALLOTT. Mathews.

PHILIPS. Mathews ... (*Adjusts it slightly.*) Right ... (*Glances round.*) See you.

ALLOTT. See you.

(PHILIPS *looks round once more: nods: goes.*

ALLOTT *stays precisely where he is, standing.*

*Long pause.*

*In the silence, eventually,* STELLA *comes in.*)

STELLA. No one here?

ALLOTT. We're ready.

STELLA. Want me up?

ALLOTT. Pose.

(STELLA *climbs on to the throne: disrobes. Stands there. Then:*)

STELLA. How do you want me?

ALLOTT. Natural.

(STELLA *poses.*)

STELLA. Where are the others?

ALLOTT. Coming.

(SAUNDERS *enters. Moves round self-consciously in duffle-coat, board beneath his arm: considers which of the donkeys he might take.*)

SAUNDERS. Snowing.

ALLOTT. Really?

SAUNDERS. Outside ... Stella.

STELLA. Hello, Samuel.

SAUNDERS. The name's Terry. Samuel or Sammy is a nickname given me by the students.

STELLA. I'm sorry, Terry.

SAUNDERS. Do you mind if I sit here?

STELLA. Keep an eye on you.

SAUNDERS. I prefer to see your face ... I don't like human beings to be set down as objects ... Are you drawing as well, Mr Allott?

ALLOTT. I ... create, Saunders, in an altogether different dimension.

(SAUNDERS *settles himself. Pause. Then*:)

SAUNDERS. The human condition ... is made up of many ambivalent conditions ... that's one thing I've discovered ... love, hatred ... despair, hope ... exhilaration, anguish ... and it's not these conditions themselves that are of any significance but the fact that, as human beings, we oscillate between them ... It's the oscillation between hope and despair that's the great feature of our existence, not the hope, or the despair, in themselves.

(*Pause.*)

STELLA. It's a wonderful observation ...

(*Pause.* SAUNDERS *settles himself: gets out his equipment.*) I like people who think about life.

SAUNDERS. I don't think about life. I'm merely interested in recording it.

STELLA. I see.

(SAUNDERS *sets up his plumb-line and strings, etc., facing* STELLA.)

SAUNDERS. I think Mr Allott is quite correct: all great art is

74

truly impersonal. All great *lives* are impersonal ... To live truly you have to be ...

ALLOTT. Impersonal.

SAUNDERS. It's only the disinterested person who sees what's truly there. I learnt that from you, sir.

ALLOTT. Yes.

SAUNDERS. These others have no regard for anything ... They have no *conception* of those qualities which can lift a man above his habitual animal existence.

ALLOTT. No.

SAUNDERS. Can you lift your head a bit higher, Stella ...

STELLA. Like this?

SAUNDERS (*examines her for a while in silence. Then:*) Yes.

> (*Roar outside:* MATHEWS, WARREN, MOONEY, GILLIAN, BRENDA *and* CATHERINE *enter in a noisy group.* WARREN: 'All over the bloody floor!' *Laughter.*)

GILLIAN. We've started.

ALLOTT. To your donkeys, men ...

> (MATHEWS *blows raspberry. Laughter.*)

CATHERINE. Sir! It's a new one.

BRENDA. The light's all different.

ALLOTT. Sufficient unto the day is the evil thereof, Catherine.

CATHERINE. Sir! I've got to start all over again ...!

WARREN. Improvise.

ALLOTT. Improvisation is the hallmark of the bereft imagination ... Draw, Catherine ... Brenda ... Warren ... Carter ... Mathews ... Mooney ... Gillian ... Draw. Register, merely, what you see before you.

> (MATHEWS *blows raspberry: laughter.*)

WARREN (*calling*). How are you, Sammy?

SAUNDERS. All right.

BRENDA. Brought your binoculars, have you?

MATHEWS. Now, then. Now, then. What have we got here?

> (*Rubs hands, gazes at* STELLA, *standing over his donkey.*)

Head, hands, feet, two tits ... a pair o' smashers ... all correct and ready to go. (*Salutes: raspberry: gets down to it.*)
(*Silence slowly descends:* WARREN *belches: laughter. Silence descends again. Then:*)

BRENDA. Quiet, i'n it?
(*Laughter. Silence grows again: snigger — muffled; titter — muffled.*
*Long pause.*)
Whatch'a have, then?

GILLIAN. Sago.

WARREN. Terrible.

MATHEWS. Never eat here.

CARTER. Go to the Excelsior myself.

CATHERINE. That restaurant?

CARTER. Snack-bar ... soup, coffee: that's all you need for lunch.

WARREN (*belches*). Go to the pub, personally, myself.

MOONEY. Can't afford it.

MATHEWS. Catering for two.

MOONEY. Piss off.
(WARREN *belches.*
*They go on drawing.*
ALLOTT *stands at the back: abstracted.*
*Silence.*)

GILLIAN. You've got a spot, Stella.

STELLA. Where?

GILLIAN. Left leg.

CARTER. Look at it *later*.

CATHERINE. Inside your knee.

STELLA. Oh ... yes!

BRENDA. I've got some ointment.

CARTER. Later.

WARREN. Later!

CATHERINE. Honestly!

(STELLA *gazes at them: resumes her pose.*
*Silence. Then:*)

MATHEWS. What you drawing, Gillian?

GILLIAN. Not you.

MOONEY. Leave her alone, fart-face.

MATHEWS (*to* MOONEY: *makes a fist*). Push this up your nose.

MOONEY. Push it up somewhere else might be more useful.

MATHEWS. Look! (*Rises threateningly.*)

ALLOTT (*stepping forward*). I thought — with your permission —
I might pose myself.

CATHERINE. Sir!

BRENDA. Sir.

CATHERINE. How super!

GILLIAN. Not in the nude, sir!

ALLOTT. Why not?

CATHERINE. Oh ... sir!

WARREN. Go on, sir ... Let em have it!

ALLOTT. I thought it might be an inducement ...

BRENDA. Sir!

ALLOTT. The sort, Brenda, of whose absence you were
complaining only a little while ago.

CATHERINE. Sir! You can't.

MATHEWS. Here ... go on, sir. I'll come up with you!

(MATHEWS *springs up on to the throne:*
*screams: roars of laughter.*
STELLA *descends, screaming: snatches her dressing-gown.*
*The girls laugh:* WARREN *shouts encouragement:* 'Go on!')

Five-minute poses. Who's gonna keep the time?

BRENDA. Stop him, sir. Stop him.

(MATHEWS *has begun to remove his clothes.*)

WARREN. Get it out then, Matty! Get it out!

MATHEWS. Who'll join me, then! Who'll join me!

(*Laughter: jeers.*)

SAUNDERS. It's the dividing line, you see, between life and

77

art ... Stella represents it in its impersonal condition ...
Mathews represents its ...

WARREN. Get your prick out ...! Here ... here, then. Go on .
Grab her.

(*Has already risen: seizes* STELLA *and forces her back,
struggling, to the throne.*
*Laughter.*)

MATHEWS. Here, come on, let's have a hold as well!

(*They struggle with the screaming* STELLA *between them.*)

CATHERINE. Sir ...! Stop him, sir!

WARREN. Go on, then ... Get it out, then, Mathews ... get
it in.

MATHEWS. I can't ... I can't ...

(*Laughter.*)

WARREN. Lie still, for God's sake ...

STELLA. Get off ... (*Screaming.*) Get off!

WARREN. Get it in, for God's sake.

MATHEWS. I am. I am.

STELLA. Get off ... Get off ... Get him off.

WARREN. Go on: thump it. Thump it.

MATHEWS. I am! ... I am! (*Still struggling to straddle* STELLA.)

(STELLA *laughs, half-screams at* MATHEWS' *efforts.*
ALLOTT *stands, pausing, halfway between the donkeys and
the throne.*
SAUNDERS *gazes transfixed.*
CARTER *calls out encouragement, laughing.*
GILLIAN *gazes blank, uncomprehending.*
MOONEY *has stepped forward as if he might intervene.*
BRENDA's *got up: crossed halfway and stays there.*
CATHERINE *stays sitting, her pen still in her hand.*)

WARREN. Get it in ... Get it in ... thump it, Mathews ...
thump it ...

MATHEWS. Hold her! Hold her!

STELLA. Get off ... Get him off.

WARREN. Get your legs open, Stella.

STELLA. Get him off.

WARREN. Get it in, for God's sake.

STELLA. No ... No ...

MATHEWS. I am! ... I am! ... Oh God ... Here! ...! It's lovely.

CATHERINE. Sir! Sir!

WARREN. Thump it!

MATHEWS. *I am! I am!*

BRENDA. Sir ... For God's sake, sir ...

CATHERINE. Fetch Mr Foley!

WARREN. Thump it! Thump it ... Go on, Matt ... Here. Come on ... let's have a go!

GILLIAN. Sir! Tell him to stop it. Sir! ... Tell him!

WARREN. Here ... here ... Come on. Let's have it!

MATHEWS. I'm coming ... I'm coming! ... God ... Oh God ... I'm coming ...! Hold her ... Hold her.

STELLA. No ... *No!*

CATHERINE. Sir! Sir! For God's sake, sir!

MATHEWS. Oh! (*Falls, moaning, over her. Moans: his movements slow. Slows: stillness.*)

WARREN. Jesus ... Look ... He has, an' all ... Bloody hell. Didn't think he had it in him. Cor blimey, Mathews ... (*Laughs.*)

> (CATHERINE *sits dumbfounded.*
> GILLIAN *has covered her face with her hands.*)

MOONEY. Jesus ... (*Turns to* CARTER.)

CARTER. *The dirty bugger.*

MOONEY. *The dirty sod.*

> (SAUNDERS *still sits there, dazed.*
> CARTER *hasn't moved.*
> WARREN *stands by the throne, contemplating* MATHEWS, *seemingly incredulous: stoops over* STELLA *finally.*)

WARREN. You all right, Stell?

(BRENDA *still sits there, gazing at* STELLA.

MATHEWS, *bowed, raises his head: gazes at the others: smiles; then, straightening, he breaks into laughter.*

WARREN *breaks into laughter: dances down from platform.*)
Had you! Had you ...! Thought he had ...! (*Dances in front of* BRENDA, CATHERINE.)

(MATHEWS *sits, cross-legged on the platform, laughing.*)
Thought he'd had her, didn't you, love!

BRENDA. You dirty filthy beast. Disgusting ... (*To* ALLOTT) It's disgusting, sir.

WARREN. She thought you'd had it in there, Mathews. (*To* BRENDA) Give us something to go home with, love.

CATHERINE. How could you! Let him do it, sir!

WARREN. Had her going. Didn't we, love!

BRENDA. Piss off.

MATHEWS. Stick of dynamite. (*Flourishes himself: fanfare.*)
(WARREN *and* MATHEWS *laugh.*)

ALLOTT. If you wouldn't mind ... Stella ... (*Invites her to resume her pose.*)

WARREN (*to* STELLA). Lit her fuse then, have we, love?

STELLA. Get off!

GILLIAN. I think it was obscene, vulgar and disgusting.

WARREN. It's the on'y three words she bloody knows.

CATHERINE. Why did you let him do it, sir? Why did you start him off?

(ALLOTT *gazes at them.*

MATHEWS *has climbed down from the throne, straightening his clothes, laughing.*)

ALLOTT. My own effort was to have been altogether less sensational ... That's to say, dispassionate ... (*Quieter*) ... I would have posed for you quite gladly ... as it is ...

CATHERINE. Here ... are you all right, sir?

ALLOTT. The essence of any event, Catherine ... is that it should be ... indefinable. Such is the nature ... the

ambivalence — as Saunders so aptly described it — of all
human responses ... love, hate ... anguish ... hope? Was
it hope you made a corollary of anguish ...? Far be it
from me to intrude ... my domestic circumstance ... my
personal life is my own affair ... can play no part in what,
to all intents and purposes, may well be happening here ...
a personal element which, despite all my efforts, I cannot
... understandably ... Restrain ... thorn within the
flesh ... The prospect of presenting myself to you, even
now, in what may be described as a human condition
isn't all that repellent to me ... It's merely that ... it would
no longer be, as it were, a work of art ... merely ... another
aspect of a human being.

(*Pause. Then:*)

I suppose the best solution ... Warren ... Mathews ... is
to return to the job in hand ... I to instruct; you to be
instructed ... Stella.

(STELLA *looks round:*

MATHEWS *and* WARREN *have returned to their donkeys:
silence.*

ALLOTT *straightens the throne: positions and straightens
the white cloth: pauses: waits.*

STELLA, *after a moment's hesitation, climbs up: glances
at the students; disrobes: takes up her pose.*

*Then, in the silence:*)

SAUNDERS. Head to the left, Stella ... Arm ...

(STELLA *follows* SAUNDERS' *instructions.*)

That's right.

ALLOTT. If you'd resume your various ... and singularly
varied ...

(*Pause.*

*They begin to draw.*)

No work of art is complete without a personal statement.
After all, the tradition we're ostensibly working in here is

one which declares art to be a residual occupation ... that is to say, it leaves objects—certain elements of its activity—behind ... stone, paint, canvas ... bronze ... paper ... carbon ... a synthesis of natural elements convened by man ... whereas we, elements as it were of a work ourselves, partake of existence ... simply by being what we are ... expressions of a certain time and place, and class ... defying ... hope ... defying anguish ... defying, even, definition ... more substantial than reality ... stranger than a dream ... figures in a landscape ... scratching ... scraping ... rubbing ... All around us ... our rocky ball ... hurtling through time ... Singing ... to no one's tune at all.

(*Fade.*
*Dark.*)

## Scene 2

*Light comes up: as before: throne, donkeys, heaters, easels, screens: empty. After a while* BRENDA *comes in: coat on, canvas bag.*

BRENDA. Gone.

(CATHERINE *enters: coat, cap, bag.*)

CATHERINE. No use waiting.

BRENDA. Hang on.

(*She goes to upstage screen:*

SAUNDERS *enters: coat on, scarf.*)

SAUNDERS. Hey: what're you doing?

BRENDA. Piss off.

(BRENDA *brings out* STELLA's *bags from behind the screen.*)

CATHERINE. Has Mr Allott gone?

SAUNDERS. He's in Foley's office.

BRENDA. You report it, Sammy? (*Hands one of the bags to* CATHERINE.)

SAUNDERS. Somebody's got to be responsible for decency and order.

CATHERINE. Lose his job, I shouldn't wonder.

BRENDA. Pity somebody, Saunders, didn't lose something else.

SAUNDERS. Allott's trouble is that he's got no discipline. He lets his theories run away with him. Art and life, in that respect, are separate things. No one should allow life to monopolize art: and similarly no one should allow art to be engulfed by life.

BRENDA. You in charge in here?

(SAUNDERS *has begun to straighten the donkeys: takes white sheet from the throne: begins to fold it.*)

SAUNDERS. It would have been reported in any case. I'm not averse to taking on that responsibility. Somebody has to do it. Even if it puts them in bad odour with everybody else ... They'll need this place, in any case, tomorrow.

CATHERINE. What for?

BRENDA. Another orgy.

SAUNDERS. To create something out of chaos, Catherine ... To invigorate. Distil. Not to deprave. To illuminate. Art, Catherine, should be an example. Not a reflection. If life itself is degenerate then art should set ideals.

BRENDA. He *is* taking over. (*To* CATHERINE) Got your hat?

(ALLOTT *enters: coat over arm, hat and gloves in hand.*
*Pause.*
*They wait:*
SAUNDERS *goes on tidying up.*)

ALLOTT. What are you doing with that?

CATHERINE. They're Stella's, sir.

ALLOTT. She's quite capable of collecting them herself.

BRENDA. She didn't want to come up, sir.

ALLOTT. She's got two arms, two legs; there's nothing to prevent her.

CATHERINE. We thought it'd be kinder to take them down.

ALLOTT. I think, on the whole, it might be kinder to leave them here.

(*They hesitate: glance at each other: put the bags down.*)

BRENDA. We came up to say goodnight, sir.

ALLOTT. Goodnight.

(*Pause:* CATHERINE *and* BRENDA *look at one another. Then:*)

CATHERINE. Goodnight, then, sir.

(*They go.*

SAUNDERS *works, tidying.*

ALLOTT *watches a moment. Then:*)

ALLOTT. I have to thank you, evidently ... for taking the part of public decency and order in this matter, Saunders.

SAUNDERS. That's right.

ALLOTT. I thought, on the whole, you enjoyed it. Gave you something to speculate about ... All the artist needs, after all, is *meat*—something to react to, report on, comment about, differentiate between ... *record* ... he never has to act. At least, that's how I've always understood it.

SAUNDERS. Perhaps we're talking, sir, about a different kind of art.

ALLOTT. Evidently. I've lost my job.

SAUNDERS. I'm sorry to hear that, sir.

ALLOTT. So am I. I've lost a wife ... I've also lost my sole means, if it were at all desirable, of supporting her. It seems I'll have to dig deeper into my already somewhat limited resources and find what other potentialities might be lying there ... as a revolutionary and a leader of the avant-garde—purveyor of the invisible event, marching ahead of my time—it seems my already overtaxed imagination has not been taxed enough.

SAUNDERS (*looking round*). If there's nothing else, I'll go.

ALLOTT. That's very kind.

(*The room now is tidy: pause.*)

SAUNDERS. Goodnight, then, sir.

ALLOTT. Goodnight.

(SAUNDERS *goes to the exit. Then:*)

SAUNDERS. If you should ever feel the need to discuss why I acted like I did I'll always be available, sir.

ALLOTT. You better go, Saunders ... Your kindness ... positively ... overwhelms me. Any further display of it will reduce me—I can assure you, Saunders—to something very little short of tears.

SAUNDERS. Goodnight, then, sir. (*Goes.*)

(ALLOTT *stands there a moment: stiff, expectant.* CARTER *enters:*)

CARTER. I'm off, sir.

ALLOTT (*looks up*). Right.

CARTER. Sorry to hear about your difference with the Principal, sir.

ALLOTT. Scarcely a difference, Carter.

CARTER. No, sir.

ALLOTT. More in the nature I would have thought of a final solution.

CARTER. Anything I can do, sir?

ALLOTT (*looks round: donkeys in a neat row: throne straight, sheet folded*). It seems everything's been done.

CARTER (*hesitates. Then:*) Goodnight, then, sir.

ALLOTT. Goodnight, Carter.

(CARTER *nods, hesitates, then goes: laughter, whistling, cries, jeers off:*
WARREN *enters, followed a moment later by* MATHEWS: *evidently they've been tussling with* CARTER, *off.*)

WARREN. Night, sir!

ALLOTT. Night, Warren.

MATHEWS. Just popped in, sir. Say cheerio.

ALLOTT. Cheerio.

WARREN. Sorry to hear the news, sir.

ALLOTT. That's right.

MATHEWS. Any time you want a reference, sir.

ALLOTT. I'll not forget.

WARREN. You're the tops for us, sir.

MATHEWS. Every time!

> (*Laughter: horse with each other.*)

WARREN. Night, sir.

MATHEWS. Night, sir.

ALLOTT. Goodnight.

> (*They go: pass* PHILIPS *entering:*
> 'Night, Mr Philips!'
> 'Night, Mr Philips, sir!' *Laughter.*
> PHILIPS *is wrapped up: coat, cap, scarf.*)

PHILIPS. Sevens, old boy! (*Thumbs up.*)

ALLOTT. Snow, of course, could easily postpone it.

PHILIPS. Snow, old boy: hadn't thought of that ... Still.
(*Claps gloved hands.*) Ours not to reason.

ALLOTT. No, old man.

PHILIPS. Well ... See you, Allott.

ALLOTT. See you.

PHILIPS (*hesitates. Then:*) Goodnight. (*Goes.*)

> (ALLOTT *looks round: one last donkey marginally out of
> line: carefully adjusts it: lines it up exactly: squints along it:
> adjusts it once again. Readjusts.*
> *Then:* ABERCROMBIE *enters: wrapped up, no bowler hat.*)

ABERCROMBIE. Seen Foley?

ALLOTT. Some rearrangement of the curriculum, it appears,
is being considered ... as the result of certain unedifying
scenes observed by at least one member of the student

body ... as a consequence of which a somewhat more traditional form of life-class may well be introduced ... Revolution, after all, is not a self-perpetuating process ... it does, by definition, they tell me, come to an end.

ABERCROMBIE. That's right.

ALLOTT. I've always seen myself as something of a pilgrim ... a goal so mystical it defies description ... not gates, exactly, I see before me ... more nearly, Abercrombie ... (*Gazes directly at him.*) a pair of eyes.

(*Pause. Examines* ABERCROMBIE. *Then:*)

I attempted to negotiate ... true instinct of the employee ... scenes of rape ... masturbatory tendencies evident amongst my pupils which I made no attempt to discourage – if anything, according to reports, I did everything to stimulate ... bartering silence over *my* chef d'œuvre if I gave to the authorities no information about our Principal's own cloacal masterpiece – toilet seat a pedestal for one of the more lyrical outpourings of Praxiteles ... Decency in the end, Abercrombie, you'll be pleased to hear, prevailed. Mr Foley is cleaning up his toilet – leaving no evidence, as it were, behind. No artist, after all, I decided, should condemn another ... We are all, I've come to realize, *brothers* ... even if some, it transpires, have to be more brotherly than others ... Michelangelo's David and Caravaggio's Disciples at Emmaus – to name but two – were not that easily come by: they were the process of a great deal of mental pain. I shall let that anguish, Abercrombie, go before me ... Go before me and – if the past is anything to go by – light my way.

(MOONEY *enters, followed by* GILLIAN *holding his hand.*)

MOONEY. I came to say goodnight, sir.

ALLOTT. Goodnight, Mooney ... Goodnight, Gillian.

(MOONEY *waits for* GILLIAN *to answer.*)

GILLIAN. All I wanted to say, sir.

ALLOTT. Yes?

GILLIAN. I don't hold you to blame, sir.

ALLOTT. That's very commendable.

GILLIAN. It's the circumstances, sir.

ALLOTT. That's quite correct ... But then, in a way, Gillian, I created them. That, after all, is my modus operandi ... preparation ... assembly ... pound, grind, mix ... colour sublimated somewhat by the immediate surround ... partaking nevertheless—to some extent—of our ... relatively, Gillian ... unadulterated human temperament ... yours, and yours ... and ... (*Pauses: indicates* ABERCROMBIE.) his ... My next work may be something altogether less commendable ... That's to say, more ... substantial ... if not altogether more extravagant than what I appeared to have achieved today ... I shall have to see ... sans means ... sans wife ... sans recognition who's to know what I ... might rise to ...

(*Pause. Then:*)

MOONEY. We wish you luck, sir.

ALLOTT. Thank you, Mooney.

GILLIAN. Goodnight, then, sir.

ALLOTT. Goodnight, Gillian.

(*They hesitate: glance at* ALLOTT *once more: nod, then go.*)

ABERCROMBIE. I suppose I better go as well ... Anything I can do?

ALLOTT. Ahead of its time ... impossible to perceive ... the pageant is at an end now, Abercrombie ... The process, as you can see, is virtually complete.

(ABERCROMBIE *gazes around him. Then:*)

ABERCROMBIE. See you, sport.

ALLOTT. See you.

(ABERCROMBIE *nods, smiles, and goes.*
ALLOTT *pauses: sits.*
*Silence.*

*After a while* STELLA *enters: dressed for the cold: coat, scarf, gloves, beret. Nods at* ALLOTT: *goes to screen.*)

If you're looking for these, I've got them here.

STELLA. Said they'd brought them down. Looked all over.

ALLOTT. Recovered, have you?

STELLA. Think so. (*Tucking her hair beneath her beret, ready to leave.*)

ALLOTT. Violation, they tell me, is a prerequisite of art ... disruption of prevailing values ... re-integration in another form entirely. What you see and feel becomes eternal ... a flower grows ... a million million years it takes to blossom ... (*Waits.*) Will you be coming up tomorrow?

STELLA. I suppose so ... (*Checks bags.*) Shopping ... (*Examines contents.*) ... (*Looks up.*) See you, Mr Allott.

ALLOTT. See you.

*(As* STELLA *goes:)*

Would you ...

*(She pauses, turning:)*

... put out the light?

*(Pauses: nods: she goes: a moment later the light diminishes.* ALLOTT *stands: pulls on his coat: puts on his hat.* FOLEY *enters in the half-light.*)

FOLEY. Still here, are you.

*(Pause: he gazes round.)*

ALLOTT. That's right.

*(*FOLEY *gazes overhead for a while. Then:)*

FOLEY. Thought of writing one up myself. (*Nods at wall.*) 'When is a man not a man?'

*(Pause.)*

I could never think of a second line.

ALLOTT. That's right.

FOLEY. It's not without some regret ... (*Gestures to him.*) You leaving.

ALLOTT. No.

FOLEY. I hope you'll find your next appointment more rewarding.

ALLOTT. I don't know ... It's had its compensations, Principal ... I've achieved some of my best work, I think, in here.

FOLEY. I believe in forgiveness, Allott ... Apart from a good digestion, it's the one indispensable principle of human growth.

ALLOTT. That's right.

FOLEY. A man—if he puts his mind to it—can always mend his ways. Experience, you see, can put you right ... In here, the mind atrophies, hardens: when the soul is constipated it means the nourishment isn't right.

ALLOTT. I'll keep my bowels open.

FOLEY. It'll make a difference, I can tell you that ... You'll leave the life-room tidy? (*Waits for* ALLOTT's *acknowledgment.*) Set an example, otherwise no one follows. (*Puts out his hand.*) I better say goodnight.

ALLOTT. Goodnight, Principal. (*Shakes his hand.*)

   (FOLEY *looks round, briskly: nods: he goes.*
   ALLOTT *looks round: draws on his gloves: pulls up his collar: looks round once again, freshly: goes.*
   *Fade.*)